The Ancient

# Dead Sea Scroll

# Calendar

## AND THE PROPHECIES IT REVEALS

By Ken Johnson, Th.D.

The Ancient Dead Sea Scroll Calendar
by Ken Johnson, Th.D.

Printed in the United States of America

ISBN: 9798617849655

Unless otherwise indicated, Bible quotations are taken from the King James Version.

Quotation from the Testaments are from the *Ancient Testaments of the Patriarchs*

2

# Contents

3

4

# Introduction

Most of us who study ancient history and church history in general, know about the modern Jewish Calendar. It is a lunar calendar consisting of a 354-day year. Its months start on a new moon and every three to five years there is a leap month to keep it somewhat in sync with the four seasons.

The calendar most of us are familiar with, and use on a daily basis, is called the Gregorian Calendar. It is a solar calendar consisting of a 365-day year. There is a leap day once every four years.

Some holidays are set on the solar calendar. The American Independence Day always occurs on the fourth of July. Other holidays are set on the lunar calendar. This is why Easter is always on a different Sunday each year. Easter is calculated to occur on the first Sunday after the first full moon occurring on or after the spring equinox.

What we were never told is that there was another calendar; a solar one, used by the Essenes. This is their story.

The Essenes taught that God gave us the perfect calendar. The base unit for the calendar was a twenty-four-hour day that was put in sets of seven, called weeks. Their calendar year was 364 days long, which was evenly divided into fifty-two weeks. This made all holidays fall on the same day of the week every year. Our Gregorian calendar shifts weekdays one or two days every year. This makes the seven-day cycle and the holidays off from year to year.

The Essenes said this calendar was observed unbroken from the time of Adam to Moses and down to the time of David. David wrote songs for each of the fifty-two Sabbaths of the year. We actually have some of those in the Dead Sea Scrolls! It remained the only calendar used by the Jews until the Greeks tried to force them to use the Seleucid Greek calendar. Unlike the 364-day solar calendar, this was a 354-day lunar calendar. It changed New Year's Day from the spring to the fall. It calculated the months, not by the solstices and equinoxes, but by the lunar new moon. To do this they had a leap month added to the calendar every three years. The Maccabees rose up and drove out the Greeks. Antiochus Epiphanes died, and the new ruler was more interested in taxes than religion. Antiochus V Eupator made a deal with the Maccabees. The Jews could keep their religion, but they had to pay tribute and use the Seleucid Empire's calendar. The Maccabees accepted the offer seeing no problem with using a different calendar. If we believe the Dead Sea Scrolls, this is the true origin of the modern Jewish Calendar. The Zadok priests said that giving up the original solar calendar alone would be a grievous sin. Eventually the Zadok priests were driven out and settled in Qumran. They took with them copies of everything in the temple library.

Now for the first time in almost two thousand years, we can recreate their calendar and see what secrets it may hold.

# Part 1
# Calendar History

# Ancient Dead Sea Scroll Calendar

# Gregorian Calendar

We should start by studying the common calendar in use today in most of the modern world. It is called the Gregorian calendar. This calendar was put in the form we have today by Julius Caesar in 46 BC. In the Middle Ages the Julian calendar became off more than a week because of the way the leap years were calculated. Pope Gregory ordered a reformation of the Julian calendar in October of AD 1582. This just changed the way the leap years were calculated. It did not change any other aspect of the Julian calendar. Unless we are discussing the leap year calculation the Julian and Gregorian calendars are identical.

**Calendar Months**
Julius Caesar started his year in the winter season.

The first month of the year is January, which has 31 days.
The second month is February with 28 days, except for leap years, when it has 29 days.
The third month is March having 31 days.
The fourth month is April having 30 days.
The fifth month is May having 31 days.
The sixth month is June having 30 days.
The seventh month is July having 31 days.
The eighth month is August having 31 days.
The ninth month is September having 30 days.
The tenth month is October having 31 days.

9

The eleventh month is November having 30 days.
The twelfth and final month is December which has 31 days.

According to the Dead Sea Scroll calendar, the year originally started at the spring equinox and the months did not have names; they were simply numbered one through twelve.

Can we see any evidence of this in the Gregorian calendar itself?

**Start of the Year**
The first month would have just been numbered month one. Roman historians Titus Livius (Livy) and Plutarch record the second king of Rome, Numa Pompilius, ordered the first month to be named after the first Italian king of the empire.

*The Ancient Book of Jasher* records that the name of the first Italian king was Janeas. That is where we get the name "January."

> "And in those days died Janeas king of the children of Chittim [Rome], and they buried him in his temple which he had built for himself in the plain of Canopia for a residence, and Latinus reigned in his stead."
> *Ancient Book of Jasher 74:6*

July is named after Julius Caesar and August is named after Augustus Caesar. When we get to the last four months of the Gregorian calendar, we see something very interesting. The names of the last four months of the year are September, October, November and December. If we look closer at their names, we notice the prefixes. "Sept" means seven, "oct" means eight, "nov" means nine, and "dec" means ten. So, the ninth through the twelfth months are actually the seventh through the tenth months. This makes January the eleventh month and February the twelfth month on the old calendar.

Also, when we have a leap year, where should we put the extra day or days? They should be placed at the end of the year. If March is the first month, then the extra day should be placed at the end of February, which is what we do. It is not placed at the end of December.

**Starting of the Months**
The spring equinox does occur in the month of March, so, March should be the first month of the year. Why then does the equinox occur on March 20$^{th}$ and not on March 1$^{st}$? At first glance it may seem that the beginnings of the months are not related to the equinox at all. Each season is ninety-one days long. If we divide the season in two, we find the approximate time of the mid-season. Depending on how you divide each season the date of the mid-season can vary a few days.

Between the start of winter (December 21$^{st}$) and the start of spring (March 20$^{th}$) is February 2$^{nd}$, also called Groundhog

11

Day. Between the start of spring (March 20^(th)) and the start of summer (June 20^(th)) is May 1^(st), which is called May Day. Between the start of summer (June 20^(th)) and the start of fall (September 20^(th)) is July 31^(st), which is Midsummer. Between the start of fall (September 20^(th)) and the start of winter (December 21^(st)) is November 1^(st), which is All Saints Day on the Roman Catholic calendar and the day after Halloween. This clearly shows that the Romans used the mid-season days as the start of their months.

**Conclusion**

After looking closely at the Gregorian calendar, we can see that before Julius Caesar reformed the old Roman calendar, the original new year was the spring equinox, just as the Dead Sea Scrolls state. Julius changed the start of the months to align with the mid-seasonal points instead of the turn of the seasons.

# Modern Jewish Calendar

Now we need to compare the Dead Sea Scroll calendar with the modern Jewish calendar.

The modern Jewish calendar is a luni-solar calendar. It is based on the solar year but incorporates the moon phases for its months. This means the calendar year consists of 354 days, with a leap month, called Adar II, about every three years. This makes the modern Jewish calendar ten days shorter than the Dead Sea Scroll calendar and eleven days shorter than the modern Gregorian calendar. The modern Jewish calendar's new year starts in the fall.

The calendar used by the Pharisees in the first century was said to be based on observation. When a committee of priests would spot the crescent moon, they would declare a new month. When the Jerusalem temple was destroyed, and the nation of Israel was dispersed, various Jewish groups began to have problems keeping the calendar in sync with other Jewish groups. The modern calendar came into being in the fourth century AD, when rabbi Hillel III created the rules governing the current Jewish calendar. These changes to the calendar system move holy days so they would not fall on Sabbaths and other similar things.

**Calendar Months**
For the last seventeen-hundred years, the days for each month are as follows:

13

The first month of the year is Tishrei, which has 30 days.
The second month is Heshvan which has 29 or 30 days.
The third month is Kislev which has 29 or 30 days.
The fourth month is Tevet which has 29 days.
The fifth month is Shevat which has 30 days.
The sixth month is Adar which has 29 days.
The seventh month is Nisan which has 30 days.
The eighth month is Iyar which has 29 days.
The ninth month is Sivan which has 30 days.
The tenth month is Tammuz which has 29 days.
The eleventh month is Av which has 30 days.
The twelfth and final month is Elul which has 29 days.

## Start of the Year

The modern Jewish calendar starts in the fall, but the calculations for starting the new year are done by calculating the new moon closest to the spring equinox. These calculations are very similar to how we calculate the date of Easter. This shows an ancient memory that the original new year was in the spring.

There is a rare Jewish ceremony done by the rabbis every twenty-eight years called the Birkat Hachama. Talmudic tradition teaches that the sun was created in its spring equinox position at the beginning of the Jewish month of Nissan (Bavli Rosh Hashanah 10b). The Birkat Hachama involves saying a blessing for the sun and the calendar.

"Blessed are You, LORD, our God, King of the Universe, Maker of the works of creation."

14

According to the Talmud, Bavli Berachot 56-59, every twenty-eight years the sun returns to its original place when the world was created. This would be Tuesday evening and Wednesday to sunset that occurs on the spring equinox, March 20. This twenty-eight-year cycle is called the "machzor gadol," meaning "the great cycle."

The Birkat Hachama is a second witness to the fact that the original calendar started at the spring equinox.

**Start of the Months**

The first century Pharisees declared the start of a new month at the first sign of a crescent moon. The new year was calculated by observing the first new moon (sign of the crescent) closest to the spring equinox. The modern Jewish months are based on these same lunar months, but are changed according to Hillel's formulas.

**Conclusion**

The modern Jewish Calendar is close to the original Pharisee calendar used in the first century AD, but it is a modified version. That means it is not entirely accurate, even by Pharisee standards. Even though the Pharisees taught the new year began in the fall, there is evidence that shows this was a change the Pharisees made further back in time. Pharisee records show the new year originally started in the spring.

# Essene History

When we look at the history of the Gregorian calendar and the modern Jewish calendar, we see both originally started in the spring and relied heavily on the equinoxes and solstices for their calendar year. Let's turn our attention to what the Essenes of Qumran have to say about the history of the calendar.

The basic history of the calendar is seen in the *Community Rule*, *Damascus Documents*, the calendar fragments (4Q319 to 4Q394), the songs and psalms of David, and other works found in the Dead Sea Scrolls. There are also accounts of some of this material from the ancient church fathers and the Talmud. Pulling all these together they paint a fairly complete picture of what happened in what we call the "four hundred silent years."

**Calendar History**
The Essenes taught that the calendar was a completely solar calendar that started with the spring equinox. This was handed down from the beginning of time and used to calculate all the Jewish festivals in the tabernacle and temple. When the Exodus from Egypt occurred, which is the first month of spring, God told Moses:

> "This month shall be unto you the beginning of months: it shall be the first month of the year to you."
> *Exodus 12:2*

The Essenes taught that the original calendar was still in use when King David reigned; and that he wrote fifty-two songs, one for each Sabbath. The Sabbath songs have the dates in them showing which Sabbath it was and what the solar date was for each of the Sabbaths.

**Ezra and Nehemiah**

Some Levitical priests began mixing pagan practices into temple worship. This made God angry. God exiled the nation of Israel into Babylon. After seventy years of exile the Persians conquered the Babylonians. The Persian king, Cyrus, then freed the Jews in 536 BC. Under the guidance of Ezra and Nehemiah the nation of Israel was reborn. Ezra taught all the people the laws of God for the nation of Israel. The newly born nation re-entered the covenant of God. They put away all the idolatry, rebuilt the Jerusalem temple, and restored the worship of God in the original way God had commanded.

The high priests from the time Cyrus freed the Jews to the beginning of the Grecian era were:

- Joshua, son of Jehozadak (536 BC)
- Joiakim, son of Joshua
- Eliashib, son of Joiakim (~ 444 BC)
- Joiada, son of Eliashib
- Johanan, son of Joiada (~ 410 BC)
- Jaddua, son of Johanan

17

**The Grecian Era**

The Persian Empire fell to the Greeks in 323 BC. The Greek empire then split into four smaller empires. Two of these four empires claimed the territory of Israel as their own. One of these was the Seleucid Empire, which ruled from the area of modern Syria. The other one was the Ptolemaic Empire, which ruled from Egypt to the South. From the time of the split of the Grecian Empire to when the Maccabees arose is known as the Grecian Era. This era extended from 323-164 BC.

During this time period the Seleucid Empire and the Ptolemaic Empire had many battles. The nation of Israel was always caught in the middle of these wars. One solution to the constant battles was to replace all the various customs of each nation under their control and require them all to embrace the Greek way of life. For the nation of Israel this meant to abandon their practices of things like the Jewish sacrifices, circumcision, and Torah reading. On what would appear to be the secular side of things, everyone was required to use Greek money and pay taxes on the proper due dates of the Grecian calendar.

**The Grecian Calendar**

The Grecian calendar used by the Seleucid Empire was a lunar calendar totaling 354 days per calendar year. The new year began when the crescent of the new moon of October was seen. The year consisted of twelve lunar months. A leap month was added six times in nineteen years between March and April (around the spring equinox). There was also a leap month added once sometime in the nineteen-year cycle between September and October (around the fall equinox).

The first month was Dios, (the new moon of October).
The second month was Apellaiios, (November).
The third month was Audunaios or Audnaios, (December).
The fourth was Peritios, (January).
The fifth month was Dystros, (February).
The sixth month was Xandikos or Xanthikos, (March)
The first leap month was Xandikos Embolimos.
The seventh month was Artemisios or Artamitios, (April).
The eighth month was Daisios, (May).
The ninth month was Panēmos or Panamos, (June).
The tenth month was Lōios, (July).
The eleventh month was Gorpiaios, (August).
The twelfth month was Hyperberetaios, (September).
The second leap month was Hyperberetaios Embolimos.

**High Priest Rituals**

All of this was unacceptable. The temple rituals had to continue, and they had to be done in the proper manner. When Nadab and Abihu offered strange fire, they changed the ritual and God killed them (see Leviticus 10). The robe of the high priest had bells on the hem of the garment. This would let everyone know the priest was walking around and doing his rituals on the Day of Atonement. There was always a rope tied around his leg in case he did the ritual incorrectly and died by being in the presence of God improperly. If the bells stopped making sounds, those outside of the Holy of Holies could pull the high priest out without endangering themselves.

The Talmud, in Yoma 9a, has a record of high priests up to the destruction of the Jerusalem temple. The interesting thing about that list is that it shows that there were eighteen high priests during the four hundred years that the Temple of Solomon stood. But during the 420-year period of the Second Temple, there were over three hundred high priests! The first few righteous high priests served many years. After them the Talmud says:

> "…after the righteous priests the last three hundred did not live past one year (passing beyond the veil died)." *Talmud, Yoma 9a*

This seems to be saying that any high priest who tried to perform the ritual of Yom Kippur on the wrong day or in some other wrong way, died when they tried to do it. There may have been high priests who refused to perform the ritual. Part of doing the ritual in the proper manner was to do them on the proper dates. This could not be done if everyone was forced to use the Greek calendar system.

From the beginning of the Grecian era to the rise of the Maccabees, the high priests were:

- Onias I (~ 309-265 BC)
- Simeon I (Simeon the Just)
- Eleazar (?-246 BC)
- Manasseh
- Onias II (~ 246-221 BC)
- Simeon II (~ 221-204 BC)
- Onias III (?-175 BC, murdered in 170 BC)

- Onias IV
- Jason (175-172 BC)
- Menelaus (172-165 BC)
- Judas Maccabeus (165-162 BC)
- Alcimus (162-159 BC)

The push to stop being Jewish and start being Greek came in waves starting in the time of Onais I, around 300 BC. It got so bad that most Jews stopped practicing circumcision, reading Torah, and took Greek names. We can see in the list Jason's name was Greek and not a normal Hebrew name. His Hebrew name before he took the Greek name of Jason, was Yeshua. Jason was the last of the Zadok priests to be a high priest of the Jerusalem temple. But since he betrayed the order and was betrayed by Menelaus, he had to flee Jerusalem and live the rest of his life in exile. Some of the remaining Zadok priests were led by the Holy Spirit to avoid the apostasy by taking copies of the temple library to Qumran for safe keeping. They stayed there awaiting the first coming of the Messiah.

Onias IV read this prophecy of Isaiah:

> "In that day shall there be an altar to the LORD in the midst of the land of Egypt, and a pillar at the border thereof to the LORD." *Isaiah 19:19*

He then felt that this prophecy was referring to his time and fled to Egypt for safety and asked permission to build a second Jewish temple. His petition was granted, and a Jewish temple was built in Leontopolis, Egypt. It functioned as a complete sacrificial Jewish Temple until it was closed by Titus in AD 73, just three years after Titus destroyed the Jerusalem temple.

**The Maccabean Era**
The Essenes record that the Maccabees rose up and drove out the Greek forces. They rededicated the Jerusalem temple and reinstated Mosaic law; but for some reason the Maccabees never reinstated the original solar calendar.

High priests in the Maccabean era were:
- Johnathan Apphus (153-143 BC)
- Simon Thassi (142-134 BC)
- John Hyrcanus I (134-104 BC)
- Aristobulus I (104-103 BC)
- Alexander Jannaeus (103-76 BC)
- John Hyrcanus II (76-66 BC)
- Aristobulus II (66-63 BC)
- John Hyrcanus II (restored to power, 63-40 BC)
- Antigonus (40-37 BC)

History records that about 110 BC the Roman and Seleucid Empires recognized Israel as an independent state. At that time John Hyrcanus I started a campaign of conquest to capture neighboring nations and city states and force them to convert to Judaism. Forced Gentile conversion is forbidden. He also took the title of high priest and king which was also forbidden. The Jews who felt they should follow the high priest, no matter what he says, became known as Sadducees. Even though none of them were Zadok priests, they took their name from the Zadok priestly line. The remaining Zadok priests were in Qumran at this time. Those Jews who felt the need to follow the Mosaic law, refused to support this high priest. They became known as Pharisees, or dissenters. This calmed down when Aristobulus became ruler but flared up again when Alexander Jannaeus became the next ruler. Alexander Jannaeus continued the practice of forcing non-Jews to become Jewish but went further in requiring all Jews and non-Jews under his control to start practicing some of the Levitical priestly regulations. This led to an all-out war between the Sadducees and Pharisees that lasted over eight years, 96-88 BC. Even after the war there were flair ups and sub-factions developed. Everyone claimed to be the rightful rulers and kept trying to assassinate the leaders of the other parties. The Dead Sea Scrolls say at this time "all of Israel was walking in madness."

**The Roman Era**
The Roman Era extended from 64 BC to when the nation of Israel was dissolved in AD 135. This constant infighting led to the leaders of both the Pharisees and Sadducees, Aristobulus II and John Hyrcanus II, to petition Rome to step in to restore order. Rome took control and deposed all leaders of all parties. After a time, they placed John Hyrcanus II back into power in 63 BC. After John Hyrcanus II reigned from 63-40 BC, the last Maccabean ruler, Antigonus reigned from 40 BC to 37 BC. Complete civil order was never restored, so in 37 BC the Romans appointed Herod, an Idumean, as king of the nation of

Israel in hopes that it would end the conflict. But as we see from the Gospels, it did not. The factions kept rising up and the nation of Israel ceased to exist in AD 135.

## Prophecy of Calendar Corruption

The *Ancient Book of Jubilees* gives a prophecy that at some point the Jews would make the grave error of replacing their solar calendar with a lunar one. Here is part of that prophecy:

> "For there will be those who will assuredly make observations of the moon – how it disturbeth the seasons and cometh in from year to year ten days too soon. For this reason the years will come upon them when they will disturb the order, and make an abominable day the day of testimony, and an unclean day a feast day, and they will confound all the days, the holy with the unclean, and the unclean day with the holy; for they will go wrong as to the months and sabbaths and feasts and jubilees. For this reason I command and testify to thee that thou mayest testify to them; for after thy death thy children will disturb them, so that they will not make the year 364 days only, and for this reason they will go wrong as to the new moons and seasons and sabbaths and festivals…"

*Ancient Book of Jubilees 6:36-38*

## Conclusion

The Dead Sea Scrolls describe how God created one calendar and that the Jews kept it pure by down through the ages until the time when the Greek Seleucid Empire forced the nation of Israel to adopt their pagan lunar calendar. They also record a prophecy that this would occur. The Maccabees rose to power and restored Israel's independence but never restored the original solar calendar.

If this Essene history is correct, Israel has been using a forbidden pagan version of the calendar for well over two thousand years. We can understand why the Essenes referred to the Pharisees as "sons of darkness" and their dark lunar calendar as a corruption. They referred to themselves as the "sons of light" because they used God's original solar calendar.

# The Calendar Remains Intact

Some people will say, "Ok, even if we can recalculate what day and year it is on the Essene calendar, how do we know that nothing has changed in almost six thousand years?"

That is a very important point to consider. Did the Flood of Noah change the orbit of the earth as to throw off the calendar? Were there 360 days in a year before the Flood and 365 days in the years after the Flood? Or did the number of days in a year change at another time? If so, how could we accurately calculate what time is now? How did Joshua's long day affect the calendar? What about Elijah turning back time on Hezekiah's sundial? How can we really be sure about any of these issues?

The Essenes recorded these events and took them literally. The numerous calendar records in the Dead Sea Scrolls, along with the Enoch calendar and Jubilees calendar documents, show that the Essenes believed that the calendar was to consist of only 364 days. No calendar system can be more than the total number of days in the real tropical year. A tropical year is the number of days between spring equinoxes. A tropical year has always been 365.2422 days long. The Essenes understood the pre-flood Enoch calendar year to be 364 days long and the tropical year to be more than 364 days long.

"On that day the night decreases to nine parts day and nine parts night, and the night is equal to the day and the year is exactly 364 days long." *Ancient Book of Enoch 72:32*

The Essenes also believed that Noah used that same 364-day calendar both before and after the Flood.

"And command thou the children of Israel that they observe the years according to this reckoning— 364 days, and these will constitute a complete year, and they will not disturb its time from its days and from its feasts;"
*Ancient Book of Jubilees 6:32*

If this is true, then there has been no change in the number of days in the tropical year from Creation to the time of the Essenes.

The Essenes taught the lunar Pharisee calendar was corrupt, but never said the same of the Julian calendar that had been in use in Rome since 46 BC. The only thing recorded about the Julian calendar was that it has the same seven-day pattern that the Essenes used (see the chapter entitled the *Seven Day Week* for details). This means that if we can place the Essenes calendar alongside the Julian / Gregorian calendar we use today; we *can* recreate the original calendar.

What about Joshua's long day and Elijah turning the sundial back? If the earth stopped rotating or went backward for this to happen, it would have destroyed most – if not all – life on this planet. Rather, there must have been something in the atmosphere that reflected the sunlight in such a way to cause these two phenomena to occur. This would have changed the daylight hours on these two days, but would not have affected the calendar in any way.

## Sun and Moon Signs

Mark 13:24; Revelation 8:12-13 and 16:8-11 refer to the sun's heat and darkness over a third part of the earth and the moon either being so dark it is not seen or is blood red. These could be caused by a phenomenon that blocks light in varying degrees during the Tribulation period. Scripture never says that afterwards the sun and moon will not have the same courses as they did before. Revelation 21:1 reveals a new heaven and new earth; but until then, the old ones with their same patterns remain.

There are also lying signs and wonders produced by the Antichrist that may make it *appear* that the sun and moon are coming up in different courses but apparently they are merely the Antichrist's deception.

The prophets record that these cycles will continue undisturbed. The prophet Isaiah records that in the millennial kingdom people will still be observing the same seven-day Sabbath cycle and the same Rosh Chodesh, or cycle of months. This would include the observance of the equinoxes and solstices.

"And it shall come to pass, that from one new moon to another, and from one sabbath to another, shall all flesh come to worship before Me, saith the LORD."
*Isaiah 66:23*

The prophet Ezekiel predicted these cycles would be observed again in the millennial temple.

"Thus saith the Lord GOD; The gate of the inner court that looketh toward the east shall be shut the six working days; but on the sabbath it shall be opened, and in the day of the new moon it shall be opened."
*Ezekiel 46:1*

## Conclusion

Many nations invented their own calendar systems; but the courses of the sun, moon, and stars did not change. Enoch's prophecy states they do not change until the new heaven and the new earth. This means we can put the original calendar back together!

"He showed me exactly how the astrological laws work in regard to all the years of the world, till the new creation is made which endures for all eternity."
*Ancient Book of Enoch 72:1b*

Ancient Dead Sea Scroll Calendar

# Part 2
# The Calendar Year

Ancient Dead Sea Scroll Calendar

# The Seven-Day Week

The heart of the calendar is the seven-day week. Moses recorded in Genesis that God created the cycle of seven days at creation. Genesis chapter one lists what God created on each of the first six days.

First Day – Light
Second Day – Atmosphere
Third Day – Dry Land and Plants
Fourth Day – Sun, Moon, and Stars
Fifth Day – Fish and Fowls
Sixth Day – Land Animals and Man

God rested on the seventh day. Modern Jews refer to this as a Sabbath, or Sabbos. God also sanctified the Sabbath. This means it is set apart for a special purpose.

"And on the seventh day God ended His work which He had made; and He rested on the seventh day from all His work which He had made. And God blessed the seventh day, and sanctified it: because that in it He had rested from all His work which God created and made." *Genesis 2:2-3*

If they observe a Sabbath every seven days, then that is the basis of the calendar system. We are told that the ancient Jews did not name their days except for the day of rest, which they called the Sabbath. They numbered the days one through six and then had the Sabbath.

> "And God said, Let there be lights in the firmament of the heaven to divide the day from the night; and let them be for signs, and for seasons, and for days, and years: And let them be for lights in the firmament of the heaven to give light upon the earth: and it was so. And God made two great lights; the greater light to rule the day, and the lesser light to rule the night: He made the stars also. And God set them in the firmament of the heaven to give light upon the earth, And to rule over the day and over the night, and to divide the light from the darkness: and God saw that it was good. And the evening and the morning were the fourth day." *Genesis 1:14-19*

This special purpose was to rest one day out of the week, but it also was to be the basis for the world calendar. Josephus wrote in his history that there was a time when all nations observed a seven-day cycle in their calendar, but they never observed the Jewish rituals. This tells us that the original God-given calendar consisted of a seven-day week. The Romans changed this to an eight-day cycle but then it was changed back into a seven-day cycle by Julius Caesar in 46 BC.

> "There is not any city of the Grecians, nor any of the barbarians, nor any nation whatsoever, whither our custom of resting on the seventh day hath not come, but our fasts and lighting up lamps, and many of our

prohibitions as to our food, are not observed..."
Josephus, *Against Apion 2.40*

| Creation Week | | | | | | |
|---|---|---|---|---|---|---|
| Sun | Mon | Tue | Wed | Thu | Fri | Sat |
| | | | sun, moon, & stars | | | |

The Essenes and Pharisees both taught that the seven days of Creation were the very first week. If they are correct, then the day we call Sunday would be the first day of creation, which is when God created the light. Monday would have been the creation of the atmosphere. Tuesday would have been the creation of the dry land. The sun, moon, and stars would have been created on Wednesday. With this in mind, we can see why the Essenes start their year on a Wednesday. The fourth day of the week would have been the first day a solar calendar could start.

**Have the Days of the Week been Changed?**
Before we go any further, we need to find out if it can be proven that the fourth day of the week that the ancients observed on their calendar is the same fourth day of the week that we observe today. If it is, then our Saturday Sabbath is still Saturday. If not, then the real Saturday Sabbath might be on a Tuesday or Friday, for instance. We do not need to go all the way back to Creation to find out. Since the Essenes held their calendar so sacred and believed that the Pharisees corrupted the calendar by going on moon phases, they made numerous comments about all

35

the things the Pharisees did wrong on their calendar, repeatedly calling them the sons of darkness for following a lunar calendar. That being the case we can assume that the Essenes and Pharisees in Jesus' day kept the same seven-day pattern for their week. They had the same weekly Sabbaths or that would have been listed as yet another Pharisee error.

The Dead Sea Scrolls record that Noah commanded all of his children to observe the solstices and equinoxes as days of remembrance of the Flood, the coming judgment, and to walk in holiness toward the Lord. See the next chapter for details.

The Romans had turned the ancient winter solstice observance into a pagan festival called Saturnalia. The word comes from the word Saturn. Today that word is used as a name of one of the planets in our solar system, but anciently it simply meant "rest." This was the festival of rest held at the end of the Roman year. Romans were to refrain from working during the seven-day holiday. In ancient Roman records the Jews were made fun of because they kept the seventh day of their cycle as a day of rest. The Romans referred to the Jews as keeping their own Saturnalia, or rest, on the seventh day of each week. See Tacitus *Histories. 5.4* and Justin, *History and Origins of the Entire World and All of its Lands 36.2* for details.

The Roman calendar was originally a seven-day cycle that was changed into an eight-day cycle for a time. Julius Caesar created the Julian calendar in 46 BC. This is identical to the weekday structure used in the modern Gregorian calendar.

If the Essenes and Pharisees observed the same Sabbath and the Romans recorded their day of rest was the weekly Saturday, then we can be assured that the Sabbath has not changed from Creation up to the first century AD.

But has it changed since 46 BC? The only time it might have changed was when the world switched from the Julian calendar to the Gregorian calendar. The Julian calendar used a leap day every four years. Doing it this way, the spring equinox drifted away from the beginning of spring by eleven days by the Middle Ages. Pope Gregory authorized the Gregorian calendar in 1582 AD, which is identical in every way to the Julian calendar except the calculation of leap years. On the Gregorian calendar one day is added every four years except at the end of a century. If the century is divisible by four a leap day is added, but if the century is not divisible by four evenly, no extra day is added. As each country accepted the Gregorian calendar, they were all careful to keep the seven-day cycle unchanged. For instance, when the change occurred in America, Wednesday September 2, 1752 was followed by Thursday September 14, 1752.

**Conclusion**

After looking at the evidence we can determine that the Essenes kept what they considered to be the original seven-day cycle from Creation. We can also be reasonably certain that it is the same seven-day cycle we keep today. This means that the weekday system we use today is unchanged.

This is important since we must use the correct seven-day cycle to calculate the leap years correctly.

# The Equinoxes and Solstices

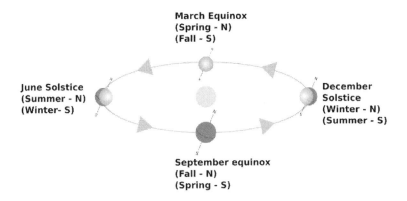

The most important function of any calendar is to mark the beginning of spring. Without this we would plant our crops at the wrong time and hunt our food at the wrong time. Eventually everyone would starve or freeze to death.

The summer solstice is the day when summer begins. It is the season of three months that are the hottest because the strongest rays from the sun are shining straight down on the northern hemisphere. The winter season is the opposite when the strongest rays of the sun are focused on the southern hemisphere making the northern hemisphere its coldest for the year. In the southern hemisphere, summer occurs when the northern hemisphere has its winter. Because of the tilt of the earth's axis, the days are longer in the summer and shorter in the winter. This adds to the cold and heat. At the winter solstice there is approximately eight hours of day and sixteen hours of night in one twenty-four-hour period. At the summer solstice it is the opposite, about sixteen hours of light and eight hours of darkness.

Ancient historical records are written from the view of the northern hemisphere, so we will concentrate on that. When the day and night is equal (twelve hours of each) that is called an equinox. On the American calendar, the spring equinox that heralds the beginning of planting time occurs around March 20 each year.

The Hebrew word *Tekufah* is used to describe the divisions of the four seasons, so Tekufah refers to both the summer and winter solstices and spring and fall equinoxes. There are four Tekufahs in all.

**The Four Seasons**
According to the Dead Sea Scrolls, Noah gave the Noahide laws to his sons to pass down to all mankind. These were to establish courts of justice and enforce moral law. The Mosaic law would come 792 years later. At the Exodus, God commanded that they stop using the Egyptian calendar they were used to when they were slaves in Egypt, and return to His original calendar, which begins at the spring equinox.

"You are to begin your calendar with this month; it will be the first month of the year for you."
*Exodus 12:2 CJB*

40

The Egyptian calendar used during that time consisted of three seasons, which were one hundred and twenty days long. Each season had four thirty-day months. After the three seasons there was an intercalary month of five epagomenal days treated as outside of the calendar year.

The original calendar consists of twelve months. Each month is divided into thirty days. This totals 360 days. The four tekufahs are outside of the months. So, we have:

- the spring equinox (1 day)
- the three spring months (90 days)
- the summer solstice (1 day)
- the three summer months (90 days)
- the fall equinox (1 day)
- the three fall months (90 days)
- the winter solstice (1 day)
- and the three winter months (90 days)

The 360 days inside the months and the four tekufahs outside of the months total a 364-day calendar year.

**Days of Remembrance**
In the Book of Jubilees, Noah commands that the first day of each season is to be set aside as a "day of remembrance."

"For I have written in the book of the first law, in that which I have written for thee, that thou shouldst celebrate it in its season, one day in the year, and I explained to thee its sacrifices that the children of Israel should remember and should celebrate it

41

throughout their generations in this month, one day in every year. And on the new moon of the first month, and on the new moon of the fourth month, and on the new moon of the seventh month, and on the new moon of the tenth month are the days of remembrance, and the days of the seasons in the four divisions of the year. These are written and ordained as a testimony forever."
*Ancient Book of Jubilees 6:22-23*

These days are set aside as holidays where the family leaves their work and comes together for a feast. They remember the Flood and practice repentance. They also study the writings of the prophets.

**Three Calendar Types**
All the ancient nations knew that the tropical year was about 365.25 days long, but you cannot create a calendar with a partial day.

The Gregorian calendar has a 365-day calendar and adds a leap day every four years. This is the most accurate way to calculate the seasons, but it causes the seven-day Sabbath cycle, to start on a different day each year. It also causes the moon phases to occur on different days throughout each year. We do this because the seasons are the most important part of the calendar to us. The Sabbath and moon cycles are not needed for the Gregorian system.

The Dead Sea Scroll calendar has a 364-day year, because the seasons and the seven-day Sabbath cycle were equally important to the Essenes. They did not care about the moon phases.

The Pharisee calendar was a 354-day luni-solar one. They needed to keep track of the seven-day Sabbath cycle and the seasons; but the moon phases were of utmost importance. They began each month on the new moon. To do this they had to start their first month of the year on the new moon closest to the equinox and about every three years they would have to add a leap month.

## Gilgals

Gilgal is a Hebrew word meaning circle of standing stones. There were several of them. If it was cloudy on the day of the spring equinox and the date could not be verified from the tabernacle or temple, it could always be verified from a gilgal. A gilgal is similar to Stonehenge. If the circle of standing stones was large enough, it could be used to pinpoint the exact day of the year. There still exists a gilgal called Gilgal Rephaim in the Golan heights area of northern Israel. Gilgal Rephaim still works well. On the summer solstice light shines down into the center chamber of the gilgal. This only happens on that one day of the year.

Gilgal Rephaim by Abraham Graicer, 2010; courtesy Wikipedia

The kings of Israel would always meet the prophets at a gilgal on the high Sabbaths (festival days) and on the heads of the months.

> "Send me, I pray thee, one of the young men, and one of the asses, that I may run to the man of God, and come again. And he said, Wherefore wilt thou go to him today? it is neither new moon [Rosh Chodesh or head of the months], nor sabbath." *2 Kings 4:22-23*

Remember that the apostle Paul stated that the Gentiles are not obligated to observe these customs, but we are free to learn about them.

"Let no man therefore judge you in meat, or in drink, or in respect of an holyday, or of the new moon, or of the sabbath days: Which are a shadow of things to come; but the body is of Christ." *Colossians 2:16-17*

**Dead Sea Scroll Sundial**

Sundials were found in Qumran. When examined carefully, we can see how they used these sundials to mark the exact day of the summer and winter solstices and the spring and fall equinoxes. The sundials are round and have a gnomon in the center to cast a shadow. There are seven circles embossed on the sundial. The circles mark equinoxes, solstices, and months. When the sundial is set

45

at the proper angle and the end of the shadow sets exactly on the specific circle, it indicates that the equinox or solstice as arrived.

Shadow on the summer solstice     Shadow on the fall equinox

Shadow on the winter solstice     Shadow on the spring equinox

# The Essene Year

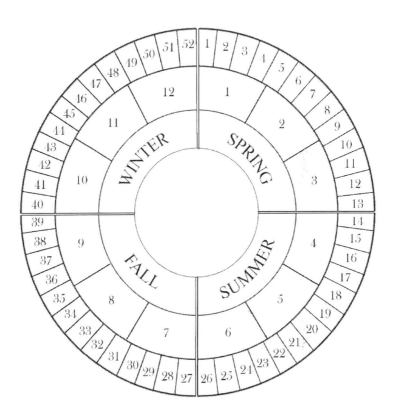

### The Seasonal Pattern

The divisions of the year are grouped into four seasons, starting with spring, then summer, fall, and finishing with winter. The spring season would be marked with the spring equinox. The equinoxes and solstices are named after the months that start the seasons. The spring equinox is called Tekufah Nisan. The day after the spring equinox is the first day of spring and New Year's Day. This would be the first of Nisan, or the first day of the first month. Each month would consist of thirty days each. After the three spring months, the ninety-first day of the year, would mark the summer solstice called Tekufah Tammuz. The following day is the first day of Summer. This is the first of Tammuz, or the first day of the fourth month. After the three summer months which would be another ninety days, the fall equinox would occur on the 182 day of the year. The fall equinox is called Tekufah Tishrei. The next day would be the first day of Tishrei or the first day of the seventh month. After the ninety days of fall, on the 273 day of the year the winter solstice would occur. The winter solstice is called Tekufah Tevet. The next day would be the first of Tevet, or the first day of the tenth month. After the ninety days of winter on the 364th day of the year would be the spring equinox called Tekufah Nisan. The next day would be the start of the following year.

**The Twelve Months**
Nisan is the first month of the year.
Iyar is the second month.
Sivan is the third month.
Tammuz is the fourth month.
Av is the fifth month.
Elul is the sixth month.
Tishrei is the seventh month.
Heshvan is the eighth month.
Kislev is the ninth month.
Tevet is the tenth month.
Shevat is the eleventh month.

Adar is the twelfth month.

## Fifty-two Weeks

A 364-day calendar year divides into fifty-two weeks exactly. That means every year starts on the same day of the week; a Wednesday. Every holy day is on the same day of the week in the same month. Passover is always Tuesday, Nisan 14.

## Calculated vs. Actual Equinox

The Essene calendar scrolls show the spring equinox on a Tuesday. The very next day is Wednesday the first of Nisan. This Wednesday is New Year's Day. The following year, 364 days later, the spring equinox would be one day off. With each successive year the actual spring equinox would drift further away from the Tuesday it is observed on the calendar. This would keep occurring until a leap year which would correct it. Before figuring out the Leap year system the Essenes used, we should map out the entire calculated calendar year.

## The Yearly Pattern

The spring equinox occurs on a Tuesday, the last day of the previous year. New Year's falls on Wednesday, the first Sabbath of the new year always falls on the fourth day of the month of Nisan. Anciently Nisan was called Abib. The week of unleavened bread occurs from Wednesday Nisan 15 to Tuesday Nisan 21. The festival of the first fruits of the barley harvest is on Sunday Nisan 26. The next day begins the "counting of the Omer."

| Nisan | | | | | | |
|---|---|---|---|---|---|---|
| S | M | T | W | T | F | S |
| | | Spring equinox | 1 | 2 | 3 | 4 |
| 5 | 6 | 7 | 8 | 9 | 10 | 11 |
| 12 | 13 | 14 Passover | 15 | 16 | 17 | 18 |
| 19 | 20 | 21 | 22 | 23 | 24 | 25 |
| 26 FF-B | 27 | 28 | 39 | 30 | | |

FF-B, First Fruits of the Barley Harvest

| Iyar | | | | | | |
|---|---|---|---|---|---|---|
| S | M | T | W | T | F | S |
| | | | | | 1 | 2 O7 |
| 3 | 4 | 5 | 6 | 7 | 8 | 9 O14 |
| 10 | 11 | 12 | 13 | 14 | 15 | 16 O21 |
| 17 | 18 | 19 | 20 | 21 | 22 | 23 O28 |
| 24 | 25 | 26 | 27 | 28 | 29 | 30 O35 |

O1-49, the counting of the Omer

The counting of the Omer is a daily count for fifty days. They fiftieth day is Pentecost Sunday, which occurs on Sunday, Sivan 15. This begins the fifty-day count to the Festival of New Wine. For the prophetic significance of the festivals see Part 4 of this book, *Festivals in Prophecy*.

| Sivan | | | | | | |
|---|---|---|---|---|---|---|
| S | M | T | W | T | F | S |
| 1 | 2 | 3 | 4 | 5 | 6 | 7<br>O42 |
| 8 | 9 | 10 | 11 | 12 | 13 | 14<br>O49 |
| 15<br>Pent. | 16 | 17 | 18 | 19 | 20 | 21<br>W7 |
| 22 | 23 | 24 | 25 | 26 | 27 | 28<br>W14 |
| 29 | 30 | | | | | |

Pent., Pentecost; W1-49, the daily count to the Festival of New Wine

| Tammuz | | | | | | |
|---|---|---|---|---|---|---|
| S | M | T | W | T | F | S |
| | | Summer<br>solstice | 1 | 2 | 3 | 4<br>W21 |
| 5 | 6 | 7 | 8 | 9 | 10 | 11<br>W28 |
| 12 | 13 | 14 | 15 | 16 | 17 | 18<br>W35 |
| 19 | 20 | 21 | 22 | 23 | 24 | 25<br>W42 |
| 26 | 27 | 28 | 39 | 30 | | |

The summer solstice occurs the day after Sivan 30 which is also the day before Tammuz 1.

The festivals of new wine, oil, and wood are celebrations that have been forgotten by modern Judaism. Since Passover and Pentecost were prophetic, these other festivals must be studied to see if they teach prophecy.

51

| Av | | | | | | |
|---|---|---|---|---|---|---|
| S | M | T | W | T | F | S |
|  |  |  |  |  | 1 | 2<br>W49 |
| 3<br>FF-NW | 4 | 5 | 6 | 7 | 8 | 9<br>NO7 |
| 10 | 11 | 12 | 13 | 14 | 15 | 16<br>NO14 |
| 17 | 18 | 19 | 20 | 21 | 22 | 23<br>NO21 |
| 24 | 25 | 26 | 27 | 28 | 29 | 30<br>NO28 |

FF-NW, First Fruits of New Wine; NO1-49, the daily count to the Festival of New Oil

| Elul | | | | | | |
|---|---|---|---|---|---|---|
| S | M | T | W | T | F | S |
| 1 | 2 | 3 | 4 | 5 | 6 | 7<br>NO35 |
| 8 | 9 | 10 | 11 | 12 | 13 | 14<br>NO42 |
| 15 | 16 | 17 | 18 | 19 | 20 | 21<br>NO49 |
| 22<br>FF-NO | 23<br>WO | 24<br>WO | 25<br>WO | 26<br>WO | 27<br>WO | 28<br>WO |
| 29 | 30 |  |  |  |  |  |

FF-NO, First Fruits of New Oil; WO, Wood Offering

The Festival of New Wine falls on Sunday, Av 3. Then the count to the festival of New Oil begins. The festival of New Oil occurs on Sunday, Elul 22. Notice that the festivals of the first fruits of the barley harvest, Pentecost, new wine, and new oil all occur on a Sunday. Elul 23-28 are the wood offerings for the twelve tribes.

| Tishrei | | | | | | |
|---|---|---|---|---|---|---|
| S | M | T | W | T | F | S |
| | | Fall equinox | 1 Trump. | 2 | 3 | 4 |
| 5 | 6 | 7 | 8 | 9 | 10 Atone. | 11 |
| 12 | 13 | 14 | 15 T1 | 16 T2 | 17 T3 | 18 T4 |
| 19 T5 | 20 T6 | 21 T7 | 22 GD | 23 | 24 | 25 |
| 26 | 27 | 28 | 39 | 30 | | |

Trump., Festival of Trumpets; Atone., Day of Atonement; T1-7, the seven days of Tabernacles

| Heshvan | | | | | | |
|---|---|---|---|---|---|---|
| S | M | T | W | T | F | S |
| | | | | | 1 | 2 |
| 3 | 4 | 5 | 6 | 7 | 8 | 9 |
| 10 | 11 | 12 | 13 | 14 | 15 | 16 |
| 17 | 18 | 19 | 20 | 21 | 22 | 23 |
| 24 | 25 | 26 | 27 | 28 | 29 | 30 |

The day after Elul 30 is the calculated fall equinox. The following day is Wednesday, Tishrei 1. This is the Festival of Trumpets. On Friday, Tishrei 10 is the Day of Atonement. Wednesday, Tishrei 15 through Tuesday, Tishrei 21 is the Festival of Tabernacles. Wednesday, Tishrei 22 is the Festival of the Great Day.

Ancient Dead Sea Scroll Calendar

| Kislev | | | | | | |
|---|---|---|---|---|---|---|
| S | M | T | W | T | F | S |
| 1 | 2 | 3 | 4 | 5 | 6 | 7 |
| 8 | 9 | 10 | 11 | 12 | 13 | 14 |
| 15 | 16 | 17 | 18 | 19 | 20 | 21 |
| 22 | 23 | 24 | 25 H1 | 26 H2 | 27 H3 | 28 H4 |
| 29 H5 | 30 H6 | | | | | |

H1-8, the eight days of Hanukkah

| Tevet | | | | | | |
|---|---|---|---|---|---|---|
| S | M | T | W | T | F | S |
| | | Winter Solstice H7 | 1 H8 | 2 | 3 | 4 |
| 5 | 6 | 7 | 8 | 9 | 10 | 11 |
| 12 | 13 | 14 | 15 | 16 | 17 | 18 |
| 19 | 20 | 21 | 22 | 23 | 24 | 25 |
| 26 | 27 | 28 | 39 | 30 | | |

Wednesday, Kislev 25 through Wednesday, Tevet 1 is the festival of Hanukkah. Notice this includes the winter solstice, the day between Monday, Kislev 30 and Wednesday, Tevet 1.

| Shevat | | | | | | |
|---|---|---|---|---|---|---|
| S | M | T | W | T | F | S |
|  |  |  |  |  | 1 | 2 |
| 3 | 4 | 5 | 6 | 7 | 8 | 9 |
| 10 | 11 | 12 | 13 | 14 | 15 | 16 |
| 17 | 18 | 19 | 20 | 21 | 22 | 23 |
| 24 | 25 | 26 | 27 | 28 | 29 | 30 |

| Adar | | | | | | |
|---|---|---|---|---|---|---|
| S | M | T | W | T | F | S |
| 1 | 2 | 3 | 4 | 5 | 6 | 7 |
| 8 | 9 | 10 | 11 | 12 | 13 | 14 |
| 15 | 16 | 17 | 18 | 19 | 20 | 21 |
| 22 | 23 | 24 | 25 | 26 | 27 | 28 |
| 29 | 30 | Spring Equinox |  |  |  |  |

The last month of the year is Adar. The last day of the month is Monday, Adar 30. The next day is Tuesday, Tekufah Nisan, or the spring equinox. The following day is Wednesday, Nisan 1, or New Year's Day.

55

# Leap Years

What is not stated clearly is how to calculate leap years. We need this to finish the calendar calculations. First, we will look at all possible theories and eliminate the ones that do not fit the evidence and see what is left.

### Theory 1 – No Leap Year

The first theory is that there was no leap year, leap month, leap week, or leap day at all. The Muslim calendar is like this. It follows the moon phases and never corrects itself. If the Dead Sea Scroll Calendar did this, we would eventually have summer in winter and Passover would be in the fall. Scripture states the year always begins in the spring month of Nisan, also called Abib.

> "You are to begin your calendar with this month; it will be the first month of the year for you."
> *Exodus 12:2 CJB*

Enoch states the year always begins with the spring equinox when the daylight hours and hours of darkness are equal and that the base calendar is 364 days long.

> "On that day the night decreases to nine parts day and nine parts night, and the night is equal to the day and the year is exactly 364 days long." *Ancient Book of Enoch 72:32*

Looking at these two sources and considering the fact that the Dead Sea Scroll calendar has the solstices and equinoxes built into it proves there has to be some kind of correction to keep the seasons correctly.

**Theory 2 – A Leap Month**
This theory would have us add a whole month to the calendar every so many years. This is how the modern Jewish calendar does it. It works for the modern Jewish calendar because it is a lunar/solar calendar. This method does not work with the solar year given in the Dead Sea Scrolls. It would be twenty-two years or more before we would add a leap month to this calendar the way the Essenes did their calculations. That would make the seasons off by fifteen to thirty days before a correction. We have two witnesses against the idea of using the lunar leap month.

Before the discovery of the Book of Enoch in the Dead Sea Scrolls, the only full version we had was from the Ethiopic. The Ethiopic version mentions both the sun and the moon in the section for calendar calculations. This has led some to assume there is some lunar calculation required for the calendar. The version found in the Dead Sea Scrolls has "sun and stars" in place of the Ethiopic "sun and moon." This would indicate that we are to use *only* the sun and stars to properly calculate the calendar. The moon is only to be used to check the calculations, to ensure their accuracy.

"The sun and the stars bring in all the years exactly, so that they do not advance or delay their position by a single day unto eternity"
*Ancient Book of Enoch 74:12*

The Book of Jubilees predicted that the Jews would abandon the God-given solar year and adopt lunar calculations. This would corrupt the calendar.

"For there will be those who will assuredly make observations of the moon – now it disturbeth the seasons and cometh in from year to year ten days too soon. For this reason the years will come upon them when they will disturb the order, and make an abominable day the day of testimony, and an unclean day a feast day, and they will confound all the days, the holy with the unclean, and the unclean day with the holy; for they will go wrong as to the months and sabbaths and feasts and jubilees. For this reason I command and testify to thee that thou mayest testify to them; for after thy death thy children will disturb them, so that they will not make the year 364 days only, and for this reason they will go wrong as to the new moons and seasons and sabbaths and festivals..." *Ancient Book of Jubilees 6:36-38*

With all of this evidence I think we can safely conclude there should be no leap month.

## Theory 3 – A Leap Day

The third theory is to add a day or two at the end of the year to make the first of the year come out evenly with the spring equinox. This sounds like the most accurate way of doing it, but it would break the seven-day cycle. We can see in the calendar scrolls (4Q230-231a) the moon phases were added to the base calendar. The moon phases show· there was no leap day each year to compensate for the drift.

| Sun | Mon | Tue | Wed | Thu | Fri | Sat |
|-----|-----|-----|-----|-----|-----|-----|
|     |     |     | 1 ○ | 2 | 3 | 4 |
| 5 | 6 | 7 | 8 | 9 | 10 | 11 |
| 12 | 13 | 14 | 15 | 16 | 17 ☽ | 18 |
| 19 | 20 | 21 | 22 | 23 | 24 | 25 |
| 26 | 27 | 28 | 29 | 30 ② | 1 | 2 |
| 3 | 4 | 5 | 6 | 7 | 8 | 9 |
| 10 | 11 | 12 | 13 | 14 | 15 | 16 |
| 17 ☽ | 18 | 19 | 20 | 21 | 22 | 23 |
| 24 | 25 | 26 | 27 | 28 | 29 | 30 ○ |
| 1 | 2 | 3 | 4 | 5 | 6 | 7 |
| 8 | 9 | 10 | 11 | 12 | 13 | 14 |
| 15 | 16 ☽ | 17 | 18 | 19 | 20 | 21 |
| 22 | 23 | 24 | 25 | 26 | 27 | 28 |
| 29 ○ | 30 |     |     |     |     |     |

The priestly calendar scrolls (4Q230-231a) have a repeating six-year cycle. In year one of that cycle the first of Nisan is a Wednesday. It is also a full moon. The new moon appears on Friday, Nisan 17 and the second full moon, called a blue moon, appears on Thursday Nisan 30. The moon phases are recorded every month for six years. A close look at these calendar scrolls demonstrate no leap days in the first six years. If we added a leap day anywhere in the six-year period, the moon phases would be off.

It has been noted that 4Q230-31 do not take into account that the moon adds a day every two years and ten months, which calls into question if it can be trusted for accuracy. Dead Sea Scroll 4Q317 shows the calendar calculations with the same moon phases but it has scribal notes correcting the moon phases of 4Q319-320. All together these scrolls show that the Essenes were just using the moon as a second witness to mark time.

The addition of moon phases to the base calendar prove they did not use a leap day every year. These moon phases also help to pinpoint the year the Essenes were using for the calculations. The full moon would only show up on the same day in the same week every nineteen years. Coupling that with the spring equinox occurring on the Tuesday of that same week makes it much rarer: only once in over five hundred years.

### Theory 4 – A Leap Week
The fourth theory is to intercalate a leap week every so many years. This is the only theory left so it must be the

correct one. This would keep the seven-day cycle uninterrupted and keep the seasons in check. But how do we find out exactly when to add the leap week to the end of the year? There have been several theories proposed to answer this question.

## Leap Week Theory 1 – Shemittahs and Jubilees

In this theory we would add a leap week at the end of every Shemittah (seven-year period) and add an extra leap week every Jubilee year (every fiftieth year). At first, this sounds logical because Shemittahs and Jubilees are a major part of the calendar system. The problem with this design is that there would be a maximum of thirteen days away from the equinox before the Jubilee year, and it would still have 6.11 days after the first Jubilee year. There would have to be extra leap weeks added somewhere, so the theory is incomplete and makes the year off too many days.

## Leap Week Theory 2 – Shemittahs and Sun Cycles

Another way of using Shemittah years for leap years is to replace the extra leap week on the Jubilee with one on every twenty-eight-year sun cycle. A ritual is performed every twenty-eight years thanking God for the creation of the sun and the calendar (see the Birkat Hachama in the chapter on the Modern Jewish Calendar). Adding a leap week at the end of each Shemittah and each twenty-eight-year-sun-cycle is more accurate than the Shemittah/Jubilee theory, but it still has 5.46 days left over at the end of seven hundred years.

The calendar fragments show years one through six and then year one repeats. This may not be the case every year, but since it is the case in some years the leap weeks cannot be *every* Shemittah year.

There are other variants of the Shemittah theory, but I believe all of them allow the start of the year to drift too far away from the equinox. In my opinion, theories three to five are the only viable ones.

**Leap Week Theory 3 – Wednesday after the Equinox**
This theory places New Year's Day, Nisan 1, on the first Wednesday that occurs after the spring equinox. The idea that the spring equinox cannot be the first day of the new year is based on these passages from Enoch.

"[6]In this way he rises in the first month [Nisan] in the great constellation, which is the fourth of those six constellations in the east... [8]When the sun rises in the heaven, he comes out of that fourth constellation thirty mornings in succession, and sets accurately in the constellation in the west of the heaven... [32]On that day the night decreases to nine parts day and nine parts night, and the night is equal to the day and the year is exactly 364 days long." *Ancient Book of Enoch 72:6, 8, 32*

So, it is true that the new year, the first of Nisan, occurs after the sun has entered the fourth portal, or constellation, which is after the equinox. But it is also true that the sun enters the other portals after the solstices and equinoxes.

The solstices and equinoxes are set to occur at a predetermined time on the calendar and are off a day or two from the actual time they would be observed. The function of the leap week is to keep the start of the year as close to the spring equinox without disrupting the seven-day week cycle.

This leap-week theory would keep New Year's Day closer to the equinox than the other methods while keeping the seven-year cycle uninterrupted. If the spring equinox fell on a Wednesday, the first of the year would be seven days later, on the next Wednesday. This would allow the first of the year to drift up to a maximum of seven days away from the spring equinox.

| S | M | T | W | T | F | S |
|---|---|---|---|---|---|---|
|   |   |   | VE | 1 | 2 | 3 |
| 4 | 5 | 6 | 7 |   |   |   |

**Leap Week Theory 4 – Wednesday on or after the Equinox**

This theory is the same as theory 3 except that it is thought that if the vernal equinox falls on a Wednesday, it would also be the first day of the new year. This would allow the first day of the new year to occur up to a maximum of six days away from the equinox. This seems more accurate but there is an even more accurate method.

| S | M | T | W | T | F | S |
|---|---|---|---|---|---|---|
|   |   |   | 1(VE) | 2 | 3 | 4 |
| 5 | 6 | 7 |   |   |   |   |

## Leap Week Theory 5 – Wednesday closest to the Equinox

In my opinion, the best theory seems to be to place New Year's Day on the Wednesday closest to the spring equinox. This self-correcting method would keep the seven-year cycle intact and allow a drift of only up to a maximum of three days before or up to a maximum of three days after the spring equinox. This is by far the most accurate method.

| S | M | T | W | T | F | S |
|---|---|---|---|---|---|---|
| -3 | -2 | -1 | VE | 1 | 2 | 3 |

In the next chapter the Jewish historian Josephus will give us a clue that this method is the correct one.

## Enoch's Five, Six, and Eight Year Periods

Enoch 72:32 says that the calendar year is exactly 364 days. Enoch 74 discusses the difference in the calendar months of his system and the lunar months. Enoch says that the moon has 354 days in one lunar year. This makes 1,062 days in three lunar years, 1,770 days in five lunar years, and 2,832 days in eight lunar years. The number of his calendar days total 364 days in one solar year, 1,092 days in three solar years, 1,820 days in five solar years, and 2,912 days in eight solar years.

This has made some think years three, five, and eight are special and that they must be used in the calculation of the leap years in some way.

There are almost ten days' difference in one year. The basic principle is that in Enoch's septenary system, there are thirty-six lunar cycles every three years, sixty-one lunar cycles every five years, and ninety-nine lunar cycles every eight years. On the solar calendar you would have thirty six months in three years, but sixty months in five years, and ninety six months in eight years. So in three years they appear to be equal, but there is one extra month by the time you get to year six and three extra months by the time you get to year eight. This is without taking into account any leap system so as not to confuse readers. In other words, you would think you would see the extra month in year six but it appears in year five instead and you might think to see three extra months by year nine but they show up in year eight instead.

Enoch is simply showing how off the calendar would be if it used the moon for *any* calculation. That's all. It has nothing to do with leap years.

**Evidence for the Correct Method**

If we recap the facts from this chapter, we can see that there must be a leap year sometime, and it has to be a leap week to fit all the criteria. Out of the three possible leap week theories using the Wednesday closest to the spring equinox is the most logical.

1.  The spring equinox is the pointer for the start of the year.
2.  The year always starts on a Wednesday.
3.  There are no leap days that occur every single year.

4. The solstices and equinoxes are calculated, not observed.
5. The Wednesday closest to the equinox is a self-correcting method.
6. The priestly courses do not show any leap weeks. Therefore, the leap weeks are not counted as part of the year, in the same way that the tekufahs are not counted as part of the days inside of the months.

## Conclusion

In my opinion, the correct leap week method is keeping the start of the calendar as close to the spring equinox as possible. This is best done by placing the first of the new year on the Wednesday closest to the spring equinox. This will keep the seven-day cycle intact.

# Menorah as a Timepiece

The tabernacle of Moses always faced east. This would allow a priest in the tabernacle to record the day that the spring equinox occurred by observing the sunrise that morning.

Sunrise on
Spring Equinox

Josephus says this about the Menorah:

"Over against this table, near the southern wall, was set a candlestick of cast gold, hollow within, and being of the weight of one hundred pound: which the Hebrews call cinchares: which, if it be turned into the Greek language, it denotes a talent. It was made with its knops, and lilies, and pomegranates, and bowls: which ornaments amounted to seventy in all. By which means the shaft elevated itself on high

67

from a single base, and spread itself into as many branches as there are planets: including the sun among them. It terminated in seven heads, in one row, all standing parallel to one another; and these branches carried seven lamps, one by one, in imitation of the number of the planets: these lamps looked to the east and to the south, the candlestick being situate obliquely." Josephus' *Antiquities 3.6.7*

According to Josephus the lamps on the Menorah "imitated the number" of the planets. That might mean that they were named after the planets. Originally the days of the week were numbered one through seven, or one through six and "the Sabbath." Later, the days of the week were named after the planets. Saturday, Sunday, and Monday are obvious in English as Saturn, the sun and the moon. Tuesday, Wednesday, Thursday, and Friday are easier seen in the French language than the English language. Tuesday is mardi (Mars). Wednesday is mercredi (Mercury). Thursday is jeudi (Jupiter). Friday is vendredi (Venus).

Pagans later named their gods after the planets. So, by saying that the lamps on the Menorah were named after the planets, he could very easily be saying they represented the days of the week. The lamps could be "slanted" or turned to face either east or south. I believe Josephus has given us the Zadok priests' method of recording the day of the week that the spring equinox occurred, and thereby showing when to add the leap week into the calendar.

S    M    T    W    T    F    S

It would start with the lamps all pointing the same way accept the marker lamp pointing the other way. The Essenes used Wednesday to start their calendar because Genesis 1:14-19 records that the sun, moon, and stars were created on the fourth day of the week. Wednesday would be the middle or fourth lamp in the row. The next spring equinox would occur 365 days later, one day more than the 364-day calendar that they used. This would place the spring equinox on Thursday instead of Wednesday. So, the priest would turn the fourth lamp back in line with the others and turn the fifth lamp to mark that the equinox occurred on Thursday that year.

S    M    T    W    T    F    S

Continuing this pattern, the second year's equinox would fall on a Friday and the third year's equinox would fall on a Saturday.

S    M    T    W    T    F    S

In the fourth year something interesting would happen. The marker would naturally be moved from Saturday to Sunday, back to the first lamp on the Menorah. This would signal that the year was a leap year adding a "leap week." However, since this would be the fourth year in the cycle, it would also have an extra day (the 366th day on the Gregorian calendar). By adding this extra day, the marker would move from Saturday to Monday, instead of Saturday to Sunday.

S     M     T     W     T     F     S

The fifth year the marker would move to Tuesday, then in the sixth year it would move to Wednesday, and then in the seventh year it would move to Thursday. In the eighth year it should move to Friday but every four years we need to add that extra day (the 366th day on the Gregorian Calendar), so it would actually move from Thursday to Saturday.

The ninth year would be a normal year, it would only move from Saturday to Sunday (only one day). The marker would move off of Saturday, the seventh lamp, and return to the left side of the Menorah landing on Sunday. That means we would add a seven-day leap week. After eleven cycles the pattern repeats.

| Sun | Mon | Tue | Wed | Thu | Fri | Sat |
|-----|-----|-----|-----|-----|-----|-----|
|     |     |     | X   | 1yr | 2yr | 3yr |
| →   | 4yr | 5yr | 6yr | 7yr | →   | 8yr |
| 9yr | 10yr | 11yr | →  | 12yr | 13yr | 14yr |
| 15yr | →  | 16yr | 17yr | 18yr | 19yr | →  |
| 20yr | 21yr | 22yr | 23yr | →  | 24yr | 25yr |
| 26yr | 27yr | →  | 28yr | 29yr | 30yr | 31yr |
| →   | 32yr | 33yr | 34yr | 35yr | →  | 36yr |
| 37yr | 38yr | 39yr | →  | 40yr | 41yr | 42yr |
| 43yr | →  | 44yr | 45yr | 46yr | 47yr | →  |
| 48yr | 49yr | 50yr | 51yr | →  | 52yr | 53yr |
| 54yr | 55yr | →  | X   |     |     |     |

This would keep the calendar correct for approximately 20,806 years, until another "extra day" would add up. But, when it does, the priests could simply add an extra skip day on the Menorah and start all over. In other words, it is a self-correcting calendar. It would never get off.

This method keeps both the seven-day sequence uninterrupted and keeps the start of the new year within *three* days of the equinox. If you count the number of years between leap years using this method, it is either five or six years long. I believe this is more evidence that we are using the correct method.

## After the Equinox Debate

The method taught in this chapter only allows the spring equinox to occur a maximum of three days away from the first of the new year, three days before to three days after.

There are those who believe that the sign of the spring equinox must always be before the Wednesday which is the new year. With their method, the counting and marking of the Menorah would be the same as this one, but they would place the leap week when the marker moves from Tuesday to Wednesday instead of moving from Saturday to Sunday. Their method would allow the spring equinox to vary a total of seven days away from the first day of the new year. This is the major reason I believe the "after the equinox" method is incorrect. The seasons would get too far out of alignment. It seems more natural to have the leap week when the Menorah lamp counter goes back a week.

# Part 3
# The Ages of Time

Ancient Dead Sea Scroll Calendar

# Ancient Chronology

We can begin to calculate the years by studying the chronology in Genesis 5. Adam was created. When he was in his 130th year, he fathered a child whom he named Seth. When Seth was 105 years old, he fathered a son whom he named Enos. It does not matter how long Adam was in the Garden of Eden. We know from his creation to the birth of Seth was one hundred and thirty years. By adding the 130 to the 105 we come to 235 years after Creation. The Jews call this dating system Anno Mundi and abbreviate it as AM. Anno Mundi means "the year of the world." If we compare this to Anno Domini meaning "the year of our Lord" we can see the similarity. The year AD 2020 means two thousand and twenty years after Jesus was born. This is *if* the AD calendar is accurate. So, when we add up the years to the Flood and find they were 1,656 years after creation, we would call that the year 1656 AM. That would be accurate *if* the AM calendar has not been tampered with.

We will begin building our chronology by using the books of Genesis, Exodus, Jasher, and the Seder Olam. We should all know what the biblical books of Genesis and Exodus are. The *Ancient Book of Jasher* is a Jewish history book dating from about 1500 BC, which makes it approximately 3,500 years old. It covers time from the Creation to the death of Joshua, which is the first 2516 years of human history. The *Ancient Seder Olam* is a Jewish history book written about AD 169 by a Jew who

75

wanted to be respectful of his elders, but record accurate history and what actually happened when the calendar was deliberately tampered with.

### Adam to the Flood

Genesis 5:1-28, Jasher 1:1-3:13, and the Seder Olam 1 all record the same dates. Jasher and the Seder Olam give a total number of years from Creation to the Flood as 1,656 years. We have the following from all three sources:

Adam was 130 when Seth was born (130 AM).
Seth was 105 when Enos was born (235 AM).
Enos was 90 when Cainan was born (325 AM).
Cainan was 70 when Mahalaleel was born (395 AM).
Mahalaleel was 65 when Jared was born (460 AM).
Jared was 162 when Enoch was born (622 AM).
Enoch was 65 when Methuselah was born (687 AM).
Methuselah was 187 when Lamech was born (874 AM).
Lamech was 182 when Noah was born (1056 AM).

Genesis 7:11, Jasher 4:1, and the Seder Olam 4 record the Flood occurring when Noah was six hundred years old. This would be 1656 AM.

> "In the six hundredth year of Noah's life, in the second month, the seventeenth day of the month, the same day were all the fountains of the great deep broken up, and the windows of heaven were opened."
> *Genesis 7:11*

Notice also that the date is recorded. It was Iyar 17, 1656 AM. We have three independent witnesses, the Bible, Jasher, and the Seder Olam, that state from Creation to the flood was 1656 years, one month and seventeen days.

## The Septuagint Chronology

Just a quick note about the Greek versions of the Bible. The original Septuagint was reported to be an extremely accurate translation of the Hebrew Scriptures. Church father Origin recorded that after the Messiah's death there were at least three people who tampered with the text to remove references to the divinity and timing of the Messiah. These three began to be intermingled and soon there were numerous versions created that were missing many random parts of the text. Origin created a work called the Hexapla to show the differences between all the texts. Today we have a movement who wants to use the Septuagint instead of the Hebrew text for their chronology for various reasons. It should be pointed out that almost every copy of the Septuagint text we have in Greek differs in some way from all the other Greek manuscripts. Even Josephus gives a different chronology in his *Antiquities of the Jews*. All the Hebrew works agree in the chronology including the texts of Genesis found in the Dead Sea Scrolls. More than that, both the Septuagint and the Hebrew state that their chronology can be checked against the book of Jasher.

"and he said to teach the sons of Judah The Song of the Bow. Behold, it is written in the Book of Jashar"
*2 Samuel 1:18 LITV (Hebrew)*

77

> "And he spoke to teach the sons of Judah. Behold, it is written upon the scroll of the upright.
> *2 Samuel 1:18 ABP (Greek)*

> "… Is not this written in the book of Jasher?"
> *Joshua 10:13 KJV (Hebrew)*

> "…Is this not written in *the* scroll of the upright?"
> *Joshua 10:13 ABP (Greek)*

To my knowledge, the book of Jasher was never translated into Greek. Today it exists in Hebrew, English, and a few other languages. If both the Greek and Hebrew versions tell us to compare the text to Jasher, and Jasher agrees with all of the Hebrew manuscripts but disagrees with the numbers of the Greek text, that is amazing proof as to which set of numbers we should be using for our studies.

This is overwhelming proof that we should be using the Hebrew Masoretic text and Dead Sea Scroll texts for our Old Testament chronology. We should not use the Greek texts.

### The Flood to Abraham
One mistake people make in chronology is using Genesis 5:32 instead of Genesis 11:10 for the post-flood genealogy. This can cause calculations to be off by two years.

> "And Noah was five hundred years old: and Noah begat Shem, Ham, and Japheth." *Genesis 5:32*

Were Shem, Ham, and Japheth triplets; all born in the same year? Or was the first or last of the three born in that year? We know from the text that Noah had only one wife, Naamah. So, they were all born from the same mother and father. Genesis 11:10 records the answer we are looking for.

"These are the generations of Shem: Shem was an hundred years old, and begat Arphaxad two years after the flood:" *Genesis 11:10*

Arphaxad was born in the year 1658 AM, just two years after the Flood. Genesis 11:10-24, Jasher 7:19-22, and the Seder Olam 1 give the same chronology up to Terah, Abraham's father.

Arphaxad was born in 1658 AM.
Selah was born in 1693 AM.
Eber was born in 1723 AM.
Peleg was born in 1757 AM.
Reu was born in 1787 AM.
Serug was born in 1819 AM.
Nahor was born in 1849 AM.
Terah was born in 1878 AM.

Then we have that same problem again:

"And Terah lived seventy years, and begat Abram, Nahor, and Haran." *Genesis 11:26*

Were Abraham, Nahor, and Haran triplets? Jasher and the Seder Olam state Nahor and Haran were Abraham's older brothers.

> "Terah was seventy years old when he begat him, and Terah called the name of his son that was born to him Abram, because the king had raised him in those days, and dignified him above all his princes that were with him." *Jasher 7:51*

This means Abraham was born in the year 1948 AM. It is almost prophetic that the nation of Israel, the children of Abraham, would be reborn in AD 1948!

**Abraham to the Exodus from Egypt**
We can record this time period in two different ways from the Scriptures, Jasher, and the Seder Olam.

The long way:
Isaac was born in 2048 AM (Gen. 11:26, Jasher 8:51)
Jacob was born in 2108 (Gen. 25:20, Jasher 21:1)
Joseph was born in 2199 AM (Gen. 30, Jasher 31:21)
Joseph was enslaved in 2216 AM (Gen. 37:2, Jasher 41:9)
Joseph started ruling in 2228 (Gen. 41:46, Jasher 49:38)
Seven-year famine started in 2237 (Gen. 41:54, Jasher 50:19)
Jacob migrated into Egypt in 2238 (Gen. 47:28, Jasher 55:26)
Jacob died in 2255 (Gen. 47:28, Jasher 56:1)
Joseph died in 2309 (Gen. 50:26, Jasher 59:25)
Moses was born in 2368 (Exo. 2:2, 10; Jasher 68:4)

The Exodus occurred when Moses was eighty years old. Or in the year 2448 AM.

The short way:
The apostle Paul stated that the time from when God gave Abraham the promise to the Exodus from Egypt was exactly 430 years.

> "Now to Abraham and his seed were the promises made. He saith not, And to seeds, as of many; but as of one, And to thy seed, which is Christ. And this I say, that the covenant, that was confirmed before of God in Christ, the law, which was four hundred and thirty years after, cannot disannul, that it should make the promise of none effect." *Galatians 3:16-17*

God gave the promise to Abraham when he was seventy years old. Isaac, Abraham's seed was born thirty years later when Abraham was one hundred. Then the four hundred years of Abraham's seed sojourning in lands not their own began, resulting in slavery in Egypt.

Using either method we arrive at the date of the Exodus which was after dusk on Passover (Nisan 15) in the year 2448 AM, or the fifteenth day of the first month.

**The Exodus to the Dedication of Solomon's Temple**
This one is an easy one. First Kings records 487 years from the Exodus to the dedication of King Solomon's Temple. This places the dedication at 2935 AM. The ancient date would be the eighth month of 2935 AM.

"And it came to pass in the four hundred and eightieth year after the children of Israel were come out of the land of Egypt, in the fourth year of Solomon's reign over Israel, in the month Zif, which is the second month, that he began to build the house of the LORD." *1 Kings 6:1*

"And in the eleventh year, in the month Bul, which is the eighth month, was the house finished throughout all the parts thereof, and according to all the fashion of it. So was he seven years in building it." *1 Kings 6:38*

## The Era of Solomon's Temple

This one is a bit tricky. The Book of Jasher ends with the death of Joshua, so it is of no help to us this time. If we add together all the dates in Kings and Chronicles, we come up with the temple standing anywhere between four hundred and four hundred ten years. This is because the terms used in Kings and Chronicles can be confusing. The Seder Olam shows Solomon's Temple stood for exactly 403 years. This places the destruction of Solomon's Temple by Nebuchadnezzar at 3338 AM.

So far, we have:
- Creation: 1 AM
- Noah's Flood: 1656 AM
- Birth of Abraham: 1948 AM
- Exodus from Egypt: 2448 AM
- Dedication of Solomon's Temple: 2935 AM
- Destruction of Solomon's Temple: 3338 AM

**AM to BC**

All secular historians agree that Nebuchadnezzar destroyed the Jerusalem temple in either 586 or 587 BC. When we take 3,338 plus 587 BC we arrive at the year of Creation. Creation would have been 3925 BC.

# Prophecy of the Messiah's First Coming

So far, we have seen the date of the destruction of Solomon's Temple was 3338 AM, or 587 BC. Cyrus freed the Jews from the Babylonian captivity in the year 3388 AM or 537 BC.

Daniel 9 gives a prophecy detailing the exact time between a decree to rebuild the temple of Jerusalem to the cutting off, or death, of the Messiah.

> "Seventy weeks are determined upon thy people and upon thy holy city, to finish the transgression, and to make an end of sins, and to make reconciliation for iniquity, and to bring in everlasting righteousness, and to seal up the vision and prophecy, and to anoint the most Holy. Know therefore and understand, that from the going forth of the commandment to restore and to build Jerusalem unto the Messiah the Prince shall be seven weeks, and threescore and two weeks: the street shall be built again, and the wall, even in troublous times. And after threescore and two weeks shall Messiah be cut off, but not for Himself: and the people of the prince that shall come shall destroy the city and the sanctuary; and the end thereof shall be with a flood, and unto the end of the war desolations are determined." *Daniel 9:24-26*

The angel Gabriel predicted that from the decree to rebuild Jerusalem until the Messiah would be seven weeks plus another sixty-two weeks. During the first seven weeks (forty-nine years) the wall of the city of Jerusalem and the city itself would be rebuilt.

"And it came to pass in the month Nisan, in the twentieth year of Artaxerxes the king, that wine was before him: and I took up the wine, and gave it unto the king. Now I had not been beforetime sad in his presence. Wherefore the king said unto me, Why is thy countenance sad, seeing thou art not sick? this is nothing else but sorrow of heart. Then I was very sore afraid, And said unto the king, Let the king live for ever: why should not my countenance be sad, when the city, the place of my fathers' sepulchres, lieth waste, and the gates thereof are consumed with fire? Then the king said unto me, For what dost thou make request? So I prayed to the God of heaven. And I said unto the king, If it please the king, and if thy servant have found favour in thy sight, that thou wouldest send me unto Judah, unto the city of my fathers' sepulchres, that I may build it. And the king said unto me, (the queen also sitting by him,) For how long shall thy journey be? and when wilt thou return? So it pleased the king to send me; and I set him a time." *Nehemiah 2:1-6 KJV*

Nehemiah 2:1 recorded that the decree to restore and rebuild Jerusalem occurred in the month of Nissan in the twentieth year of the reign of the Persian king, Artaxerxes.

85

Encyclopedia Britannica gives the date Artaxerxes Longimanus took the Persian throne as July of 465 BC. Therefore, his twentieth year began in July of 445 BC. The month of Nissan following that would have been in March of 444 BC, which occurred before the twenty-first anniversary of Artaxerxes' reign. The seven weeks, or forty-nine years, ran from Artaxerxes' decree to the year Jerusalem's wall and moat were finished in the period of Ezra and Nehemiah. From that time another sixty-two weeks went by until the Messiah was "cut off," a term meaning "executed."

**Messiah's Death ~ AD 32**

In the early third century, ancient church father Julius Africanus wrote a book entitled, *"On the Weeks and This Prophecy."* Only fragments remain today; but in fragment 16, he tells us how to calculate the exact date by converting the years to days and changing them from the Jewish prophetical calendar to the Roman calendar used in his day. Julius says that the "seventy weeks" prophecy of Daniel 9 started when Artaxerxes gave the decree in his twentieth year. Years later, Sir Robert Anderson recreated the conversion process for our modern calendar as follows: first, the sixty-nine weeks of years ends with the Messiah's death. If we multiply 69 times 7 this gives us the 483 prophetic years between Artaxerxes' decree and the death of the Messiah.

We convert from the Jewish/prophetic calendar to the Gregorian/Roman calendar this way: we take the 483 years times 360 days per year (the sacred Jewish calendar) and

86

that equals 173,880 days. The 173,880 days on the modern calendar comes out to be 476 years and 21 days (476 x 365.25 = 173,859 and 173,880-173,859 = 21). March 14, 444 BC plus 476 years comes out to be March 14, AD 31. We add one year because there was no "0" year between AD and BC. We then add the 21 days. The final date arrives at April 6, AD 32!

## 70 Weeks Prophecy

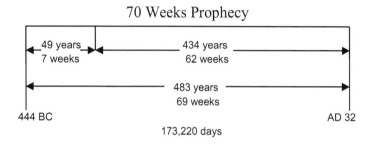

The ancient rabbis agreed Daniel accurately gave the date for the Messiah's coming. They simply say something was supposed to happen, but it did not occur.

**Ancient Rabbis Agree on the Coming of Messiah**

When witnessing to Jews, most will say Daniel's 70 weeks prophecy has nothing to do with the Messiah; but the ancient rabbinical writings, including the Talmud, state the prophecy *does* refer to King Messiah. Please point out to them that the Messiah, whoever he was, had to have come before the destruction of the Temple in AD 70. If the Messiah was not Jesus Christ, then who was he? Here is a small list of quotes from the ancient rabbis about this passage in Daniel:

"Daniel has elucidated to us the knowledge of the end times. However, since they are secret, the wise [rabbis] have barred the calculation of the days of Messiah's coming so that the untutored populace will not be led astray when they see that the End Times have already come but there is no sign of the Messiah." *Maimonides: Igeret Teiman, Chapter 3*

"The anointed King is destined to stand up and restore the Davidic Kingdom to its antiquity, to the first sovereignty. He will build the Temple in Jerusalem and gather the strayed ones of Israel together. All laws will return in his days as they were before: Sacrificial offerings are offered and the Sabbatical years and Jubilees are kept, according to all its precepts that are mentioned in the Torah. Whoever does not believe in him, or whoever does not wait for his coming, not only does he defy the other prophets, but also the Torah and Moses our teacher... Bar Kokhba claimed that he was King Messiah. He and all the Sages of his generation deemed him King Messiah, until he was killed by sins; only since he was killed, they knew that Bar Kokhba was not the Messiah."
*Maimonides: Mishneh Torah, Hilkhot Melakhim Umilchamoteihem, Chapter 11.*

"These times (Daniel's 70 Weeks) were over long ago." *Rabbi Judah: Babylonian Talmud, Sanhedrin.*

"I have examined and searched all the Holy Scriptures and have not found the time for the coming of Messiah clearly fixed, except in the words of Gabriel to the prophet Daniel, which are written in the 9th chapter of the prophecy of Daniel."
*Rabbi Moses Abraham Levi*

"Similarly, one should not try to calculate the appointed time [for the coming of Messiah]. Our Sages declared: [Sanhedrin 97b] 'May the spirits of those who attempt to calculate the final time [of Messiah's coming] expire!' Rather, one should await [his coming] and believe in the general conception of the matter, as we have explained."
*Maimonides: Mishneh Torah, Hilkhot Melakhim Umilchamoteihem, Chapter 12*

"...all we need is to do teshuva until Messiah comes, for all the predestined dates for the redemption have already passed." *Talmud: Sanhedrin 97b*

"All the time limits for redemption (the coming of Messiah) have passed and the matter now depends only on repentance and good deeds."
*Babylonian Talmud: Rabbi Rabh*

Notice the rabbis placed a curse on those who would read Daniel 9 and calculate the time of the Messiah's coming to earth. They did this because it clearly points to Jesus Christ.

Ancient Dead Sea Scroll Calendar

The Daniel 9 prophecy pinpoints the dates of Artaxerxes' degree and the year of the death of Jesus Christ. When we add this information to our calendar calculations we arrive at these dates:

- Solomon's Temple Destroyed, 3338 AM, or 587 BC.
- Cyrus freed the Jews, 3388 AM or 537 BC.
- Artaxerxes' degree, 3481 AM, or 444 BC,
- Death of Messiah, Passover, 3957 AM, or AD 32

So why does the modern Jewish calendar have 5780 AM instead of 5944 AM for the AD year of 2020?

# Tampering with the Timeline

We know the Essenes teach the Pharisees changed the calendar system but did any of them try to change the years? To answer that question, we turn to the Seder Olam.

The Seder Olam is a history book written by an unknown Jew about the year AD 169. The author tried to put together a timeline of events starting with Creation up to the Flood and going beyond that up to his time. What is interesting is that the Talmud says that the Seder Olam is accurate history and uses it to prove its timeline.

### Chronology of the Persian Era

History records that Cyrus conquered Babylon and freed the Jews in 537 BC. After Cyrus there was Darius the Mede of whom Daniel predicted there would be four more Persian kings before the coming of the Grecian kingdom led by Alexander the Great:

> "Also, I in the first year of Darius the Mede, even I, stood to confirm and to strengthen him. And now will I shew thee the truth. Behold, there shall stand up yet three kings in Persia; and the fourth shall be far richer than they all: and by his strength through his riches he shall stir up all against the realm of Grecia. And a mighty king shall stand up, that shall rule with great dominion, and do according to his will."
> *Daniel 11:1-3*

Darius the Mede ruled from 536-530 BC.

Cambyses ruled from 530-522 BC.

Pseudo-Smerdis tried to take the kingdom but was executed in 522 BC.

Darius I ruled from 522-486 BC. The Jerusalem temple was rebuilt under his reign.

Xerxes I ruled from 486-465 BC. He attacked Greece as prophesied.

Artaxerxes I ruled from 465-424 BC.

Alexander the Great reigned over the Persians for only three years before his death, from 326-323 BC. Babylon fell to Alexander in 327 BC, exactly 210 years after Babylon fell to Cyrus in 537 BC. This is what we read in the Seder Olam.

> "The kings of Media/Persia ruled for 210 years total before the coming of Alexander the Great."
> *Seder Olam 30*

### The Missing Years

The Seder Olam was written to preserve the true history in its day and bring to light the attempts of certain rabbis to change dates in history. The history in the Seder Olam agrees with the Bible, Jasher, and other works up to the time of the Persian rule over the Jews. Cyrus conquered the Persian empire in 3388 AM, or 537 BC.

In the previous chapter we learned that the standard interpretation of the Messiah's death recorded in Daniel 9 was that it pointed to when the Messiah should die, but it did not occur because God changed His mind due to the sins of the nation of Israel. This does not make sense because it would cause God to be a liar. One rabbi came up with a way to fix this problem.

The author of the Seder Olam describes a rabbi named Yose who came up with an idea that the prophecy given in Daniel 9 did not point to the death of the Messiah, as all other rabbis had taught, but that it pointed to the destruction of the second temple in AD 70. But this caused the chronology to be off by at least forty years.

To fix this Rabbi Yose came up with the idea that Cyrus, Artaxerxes, and Darius were titles, not proper names. He said that they were all the same person.

The author of the Seder Olam recorded the calculations of the rabbi and then stated he changed his mind because the numbers did not match up well with other dates. Rabbi Yose's second theory turned out to be off even more. The author of the Seder Olam tried to be very respectful of his elders, but at the same time point out that they were trying to deliberately tamper with the timeline for the purpose of rejecting the Messiah.

The Seder Olam records Rabbi Yose came up with this interpretation:

> "Rabbi Yose said: The 70 weeks are figured from the destruction of the First Temple to the destruction of the Second Temple. The seven took place while they

were still in Babylonian exile. Then the one week took place while they were moving back into the land. Finally, there were 62 weeks to the destruction of the Second Temple. Rabbi Yose also said: It was 70 years between the destruction of the First Temple to the dedication of the Second Temple. Add to that 410 [420] years and we come to the 490 years of the prophecy which ended at the destruction of the Second Temple." *Seder Olam 28*

By doing this he managed to get the time of the Persian rule over the Jews from around two hundred years down to about twenty-five years.

"Rabbi Yose said: the Persian Empire continued to exist for twenty-four years after the new Temple was completed. The Grecian Empire ruled after Persia for 180 years. After the fall of the Grecian Empire, the Hasmonean Dynasty, starting under Judas Maccabee, ruled Israel for 103 years. Then under Roman rule, the kingdom of Herod existed for 103 years before the Temple was destroyed."
*Seder Olam 30*

Eventually rabbi Yose's theories with a few other modifications, became the basis for the official Jewish year. See the *Jewish Time Line Encyclopedia* by Mattis Kantor for the Talmudic account of history.

| Event | Yose | History |
|---|---|---|
| Temple built to the fall of Persia | 24 | 192 |
| Fall of Persia to the fall of Greece | 180 | 161 |
| Fall of Greece to the coming of Rome | 103 | 100 |
| Coming of Rome to the end of Temple | 103 | 134 |
| **Total** | **410** | **587** |

Years of Rabbi Yose compared to documented history

Later, when the rabbis took rabbi Yose's theories and tweaked them yet again, the calendar year was set.

The difference between these rabbis' calculations and the dates set forth in the Seder Olam is the famous 164 missing years.

**Conclusion**

The author of the Seder Olam agrees with all other Jewish history books and keeps the correct number of years past the destruction of Solomon's Temple in 3338 AM, 587 BC. He then continues to give correct chronology and makes it clear who corrupted the calendar and when. This is one of the most well-known deliberate corruptions to the Jewish calendar by those who rejected the Messiah. We can skip all the corruption by switching to the AD / BC timeline at 587 BC.

# Biblical Timeline Prophecies

There are two other prophecies we should look at that prove we have the correct dating system. We looked at the prophecy of Daniel 9 about the number of days between Artaxerxes' decree and the death of the Messiah. We learned that it was fulfilled *to the day*.

Two prophecies we need to look at, give the exact number of days between events in the distant past and the rebirth of the modern state of Israel on May 14, AD 1948. Another prophecy records that the modern state of Israel would take back the temple mount on June 7, AD 1967. This gives a direct connection between Cyrus' decree in 537 BC and 1948 and 1967. Look back at the chapter on the *Prophecy of Messiah's First Coming* for details on that timeline prophecy. These will be calculated in the exact same way.

### The Second Return – May 14, 1948
Both Daniel and Ezekiel foretold the *exact date* of the reestablishment of Israel.

> "[4]Lie thou also upon thy left side, and lay the iniquity of the house of Israel upon it: according to the number of the days that thou shalt lie upon it thou shalt bear their iniquity. [5]For I have laid upon thee the years of their iniquity, according to the number of the days, three hundred and ninety days: so shalt thou bear the iniquity of the house of Israel. [6]And

when thou hast accomplished them, lie again on thy right side, and thou shalt bear the iniquity of the house of Judah forty days: I have appointed thee each day for a year." *Ezekiel 4:4-6*

In this passage, the sin of Israel and Judah was three hundred ninety years and forty years. To symbolize this, Ezekiel had to lie on his left side for 390 days, a day for each year of Israel's sin, and forty days on his right side, a day for each year of Judah's sin. The total time then was 430 years of sin. The Babylonian captivity took up seventy years of this punishment, leaving 360 years.

"[14]But if ye will not hearken unto Me, and will not do all these commandments; [15]And if ye shall despise My statutes, or if your soul abhor My judgments, so that ye will not do all My commandments, but that ye break My covenant... I will set My face against you, and ye shall be slain before your enemies: they that hate you shall reign over you; and ye shall flee when none pursueth you. [18]And if ye will not yet for all this hearken unto Me, then I will punish you seven times more for your sins." *Leviticus 26:14-18*

Here God declares that if Israel does not repent after the Babylonian captivity, when Cyrus freed Israel, then the remaining time would be multiplied sevenfold. If you multiply 360 years by seven, you get 2,520 prophetical years. The prophet Daniel predicted this same time period in another way.

In Daniel 4, God punished King Nebuchadnezzar with insanity for seven years, in order to humble him. God had Nebuchadnezzar *act out* a prophecy, just as Ezekiel acted out his 430-day prophecy by lying on his side. In Nebuchadnezzar's case, the restoration of his kingdom after seven years is also a symbolic prophecy that illustrates that the children of Israel would be restored a second time to *their* land after seven *years* of days. Since the prophetic calendar uses a 360-day year, if you multiply Nebuchadnezzar's seven years by the 360-day calendar, you get 2,520 years – just like Ezekiel's prophecy. From these two prophets we are told the time of the second return of Israel. We will first convert the Jewish years to Roman years the same way we did for the timeline prophecy of the Messiah's death.

Cyrus issued his decree freeing the Jews and declaring the state of Israel to exist again on August 3, 537 BC. Multiply 2,520 Jewish years times 360 days per year to get 907,200 days. The 907,200 days on the modern calendar is 2,483 years and 285 days (2,483 years x 365.25 = 906,915; 907,200 – 906,915 = 285 days). August 3, 537 BC plus the 2,483 years comes to August 3, AD 1946. Add one year because there was no year "0" and the date becomes August 3, AD 1947. When we add the extra 285 days, we arrive at May 14, AD 1948!

This was the very day that the UN declared Israel to be a sovereign state!

Cyrus' Decree            War of Independence

**August 3, 537 BC**       "907,200 Days"       **May 14, 1948 AD**

## Control of the Temple Mount – June 7, 1967

Just as Daniel 4 predicted the reestablishment of the modern state of Israel, Daniel 5 also predicted Israel would take control of the Temple Mount in AD 1967.

In Daniel 5, we read of the account of the handwriting on the wall. This handwriting is an inscription prophecy with a double fulfillment. Daniel left out the first "mene" in this riddle and interpreted only the second mene, plus the tekel, and pharsin as Hebrew *verbs* which literally read "numbered," "weighed," and "divided." Daniel told Belshazzar that the words of the handwriting on that wall meant that he personally had been weighed and found to be godless. Therefore, the days of his kingdom had been numbered and had come to an end. His kingdom would be divided and given to the Medes and Persians.

"[25] And this is the writing that was written, MENE, MENE, TEKEL, UPHARSIN." *Daniel 5:24*

The double fulfillment is for the latter days. First, notice that mene is stated twice. If we take these words as *nouns* instead of *verbs,* a different

| Mene | 1,000 | garahs |
|------|-------|--------|
| Mene | +1,000 | garahs |
| Tekel | + 20 | garahs |
| Peres | + 500 | garahs |
| | 2,520 | garahs |

meaning becomes clear. If we decipher them as nouns, they

99

turn out to be names for weights or money. A mene is 1,000 garahs. (A garah is a base unit of weight like our penny.) A tekel is 20 garahs, and a peres is half a mena. "Upharsin" is the Hebrew way of saying "and Peres." So the inscription reads 2,520 garahs or 2,520 periods of time. On this night the control of the temple vessels passed to the children of Israel. Real control of the Temple Mount would be given later by Darius. The actual building of the temple would be much later still.

This prophecy tells us that from the decree Darius would give granting full control of the Temple Mount, plus 2,520 Jewish years, the children of Israel would again be granted control of the Temple Mount – but not granted the right to build the temple itself. The calculations for this timeline prophecy are exactly the same as the ones given for AD 32, and AD 1948. The 2,520 garahs or prophetic years times 360 days comes out to be 907,220 days. The 907,220 days on the modern calendar is 2,483 years and 285 days (2,483 years x 365.25 = 906,915; 907,200 – 906,915 = 285 days).

Darius's decree to grant the Jews control of the Temple Mount was August 25, 518 BC. This date plus 907,200 days (plus one year changing from BC to AD) brings us to June 7, 1967. *On this exact date* the Israelis again gained control of the Temple Mount during the Six Day War!

Darius Decree                                                Six Day War

|—————————————————————————————————|

**August 25, 518 BC**         "907,200 Days"         **June 7, 1967 AD**

**Conclusion**

These timeline prophecies are fantastic for the purpose of keeping the Dead Sea Scroll calendar accurate.

So far, we have:

- Creation: 1 AM
- Noah's Flood: 1656 AM
- Birth of Abraham: 1948 AM
- Exodus from Egypt: 2448 AM
- Dedication of Solomon's Temple: 2935 AM
- Solomon's Temple destroyed, 3338 AM, or 587 BC.
- Cyrus freed the Jews, 3388 AM or 537 BC.
- Artaxerxes' decree 3481 AM, or 444 BC,
- Death of Messiah, Passover, 3957 AM, or AD 32
- Israel reborn, 5873 AM, AD 1948
- Israel retaking the temple mount, 5892 AM, AD 1967

# The School of Elijah

Elijah ran a school of the prophets. Josephus stated there was a prophetical work called the *Epistle of Elijah* that still existed in his day. As far as I know, it does not exist in its entirety today. The Ethiopian Orthodox church has an epistle called the *Epistle of Elijah* in its cannon. If it is the original text, it is missing a lot of information. It has nothing new to teach us. However, there is a commentary on the *Epistle of Elijah* called the *Tannah Eliyahu.*

For our purposes we want to know what it teaches about the calendar. It is obvious that it has been edited by rabbis over the centuries, but it still does contain commentary about the ages as taught by the School of Elijah. The epistle taught that human history would be divided into four "ages." The first age was called the *Age of Chaos* and was a period of two thousand years. It started with Creation and ended with the call of Abraham. According to Jasher, God called Abraham in the year 2000 AM. The second age was also to last two thousand years. It was called the *Age of Torah* and was supposed to exist from the call of Abraham to the first coming of the Messiah. When Messiah came it would start the third age which was called the *Age of Grace*. This Age of Grace was also called the temporary messianic period. We are not told why in the commentary, but the Essenes believed it was because the Messiah would die for our sins at his First Coming and rule as king at his Second Coming. The third age was to last for two thousand years. After the Age of Grace there would be a *Messianic Kingdom* which would last for one thousand years.

The concept of the four ages lasting for seven thousand years is repeated afterwards in several other rabbinical manuscripts even though it goes against what is commonly taught by them, namely that the Messiah did not come.

## The Ancient Church Fathers
Many ancient church fathers believed in this concept of six thousand years of human history and a day of sabbath rest in the Messianic kingdom. This is what the weekly Sabbath ritual was to teach us. There were several church fathers who taught that the Second Coming would be in the year 6000 AM. This was because of the Old Testament chronology, the Essene beliefs, and the teaching from the School of the Prophets. Here are some quotes from the ancient church fathers about the Second Coming.

> "Therefore, children, in six days, or in six thousand years, all the prophecies will be fulfilled. Then it says, He rested on the seventh day. This signifies at the Second Coming of our Lord Jesus, He will destroy the Antichrist, judge the ungodly, and change the sun, moon, and stars. Then He will truly rest during the Millennial reign, which is the seventh day." *Epistle of Barnabas 15:7-9*

> "The day of the Lord is as a thousand years; and in six days created things were completed. It is evident,

103

therefore, they will come to an end in the six thousandth year." Irenaeus, *Against Heresies 5.28*

"The Sabbath is a type of the future kingdom... For "a day with the Lord is as a thousand years." Since, then, in six days the Lord created all things, it follows that in six thousand years all will be fulfilled."
Hippolytus, *Fragment 2; Commentary on Daniel 2.4*

"We will be immortal when the six thousand years are completed."
Commodianus, *Against the Gods of the Heathens 35*

"Resurrection of the body will be when six thousand years are completed, and after the one thousand years [millennial reign], the world will come to an end."
Commodianus, *Against the Gods of the Heathens 80*

"Satan will be bound until the thousand years are finished. That is, after the sixth day."
Victorinus, *Commentary on Revelation 20.1-3*

"In the seventh millennium we will be immortal and truly celebrate the Feast of Tabernacles."
Methodius, *Ten Virgins 9.1*

"The sixth thousandth year is not yet complete. When this number is complete, the consummation must take place." Lactantius, *Divine Institutes 7.14*

## Jubilee and Shemittah Years

Every seven years there is a Shemittah year. On this year all the debts of Jews would be forgiven. This seven-year cycle is repeated seven times. After the seventh Shemittah (forty-nine years) there is a Jubilee year. The Jubilee year is when all of the debts of the Gentile Noahides would be forgiven.

Today, it is most commonly taught that there are seven Shemittahs (forty-nine years) and then a jubilee year (the fiftieth year), so two jubilees would total one hundred years. Others have taught that a jubilee year is not separate from the Shemittah cycles. The jubilee year would be the first year of a new Shemittah cycle. This would mean two jubilees would total ninety-eight years instead of one century. Who is right?

The *Tannah Eliyahu* teaches that there are ten jubilees in a five hundred-year period called an "onah." It also teaches that there are four onahs in the ages of Chaos, Torah, and Grace, but only two onahs in the age of the Messianic Kingdom. This shows that the jubilee year is every fifty years and not every forty-nine years.

## The Melchizedek Document

There is a Dead Sea Scroll called 11QMelchizedek. The Messiah is described as God incarnate. He was to be a Melchizedekian priest, not a Levitical one.

This scroll mentions that the Messiah (Melchizedek) would come to earth and die to pay for our sin nature, reconciling us to God the Father. It then goes further to tell us exactly when this would occur.

"The captives Moses speaks of are those whom Isaiah says 'To proclaim freedom to the captives [Isa. 61:1].' Its interpretation is that the LORD will assign those freed to the sons of heaven and the lot of Melchizedek. Even those, whose teachers had deliberately hidden and kept secret from them the truth about their inheritance through Melchizedek. The LORD will cast their lot amid the portions of Melchizedek, who will make them return [or repent] and will proclaim freedom to them, to free them from the debt of all their iniquities. This event will take place in the first week of the jubilee that occurs after the ninth jubilee." *11QMelchizedek Column 2*

The Essene calendar used the Ages as taught by Elijah. Each age was broken up into four onahs, or four parts of ten Jubilees each. If we use the biblical timeline we have shown in this book, Creation was 3925 BC. This would make the third age start in AD 75. Notice that the Dead Sea Scroll stated that the Messiah would die one Shemittah (seven-year period) after the end of the ninth Jubilee of their age. If we subtract a fifty-year Jubilee period, not a forty-nine-year period, from AD 75, we come to AD 25. If we then add that one Shemittah (seven year-period) to AD 25 we arrive at AD 32. So, according to this Dead Sea Scroll the Messiah came and died for our sins in AD 32. That is exactly what Jesus Christ did!

**The Ten-Week Prophecy**

There is another Dead Sea Scroll containing an outline of human history and various predictions that occur throughout the seven thousand years. It is called the *Ten-week Prophecy*. It divides time into ten weeks. Each day is one hundred years. One week is seven hundred years and over ten weeks of time, seven thousand years. With each day representing a century and two jubilee periods it fits nicely with the Essene calendar. The ten-week prophecy can be found in the *Ancient Book of Enoch* 93.

**Conclusion**

We have learned that several of the ancient church fathers believed in the original calendar, the Essene teachings, and taught that the Second Coming would be in the year 6000 AM. The school of the prophets divided time into three ages of two thousand years each; the Ages of Chaos, Torah, and Grace. After which there would be a one-thousand-year reign of the Messiah starting at His Second Coming. Other Dead Sea Scrolls divide time into ten weeks, where each day is one century. These documents use a fifty-year jubilee cycle. All of this helps to show the consistency of the calendar system taught by the Essene community.

# Part 4
# Festivals in Prophecy

# Festival Outline

There are seven festivals given in Leviticus that were to be practiced by the Jews. The rituals performed on the festivals taught prophecy. Here is a list of the seven.

1. Passover
2. Unleavened Bread
3. First Fruits of the Barley Harvest
4. Pentecost
5. Trumpets
6. Day of Atonement
7. Tabernacles

The Essene calendar puts some of the festivals on a slightly different date than does the Pharisee calendar that we are used to. The Dead Sea Scroll calendar also adds eight more festivals that might be just as prophetic. These previously unknown holy days are:

- New Year's Day,
- the Festival of New Wine,
- the Festival of New Oil,
- the wood offering,
- Noah's four Days of Remembrance

The spring Day of Remembrance falls on New Year's (Nisan 1) and the fall Day of Remembrance falls on the Festival of Trumpets (Tishrei 1) so those four holidays

111

combine into two holy days. There is also a second Passover on Thursday, Iyar 14. It is observed by those who were unclean during the actual Passover, Tuesday, Nisan 14. We assume there is nothing new in the ritual done on the second Passover, so we do not list it here.

For all practical purposes that makes thirteen holy days to remember. In order these would be:

1. New Year's Day, the spring Day of Remembrance (Nisan 1)
2. Passover (Nisan 14)
3. Unleavened Bread (Nisan 15-21)
4. First Fruits of the Barley Harvest (Nisan 26)
5. Pentecost (Sivan 15)
6. Summer Day of Remembrance (Tammuz 1)
7. Festival of New Wine (Av 3)
8. Festival of New Oil (Elul 22)
9. Wood Offering (Elul 23-28)
10. Feast of Trumpets, Fall Day of Remembrance (Tishrei 1)
11. Day of Atonement (Tishrei 10)
12. Tabernacles (Tishrei 15-21)
13. Winter Day of Remembrance (Tevet 1)

We will start with the first one and go through the list showing the Essene theology each represented.

# Spring Day of Remembrance

### New Year's Day
New Year's Day always falls on Wednesday, Nisan 1. It was just a time to mark the turn of the year. It is listed as a holy day, but it is currently unknown if there were any rituals performed for a New Year's celebration.

### Spring Day of Remembrance
Another name for New Year's Day is the spring Day of Remembrance. Noah commemorated four Days of Remembrance. All Gentile families were to gather together on these Days of Remembrance for a feast, fellowship, and focus on the written *Testaments of the Patriarchs* and memorize prophecy. According to Jubilees, the spring Day of Remembrance marks the time when God commanded Noah to start building the ark and when the Flood was over, and the earth became dry.

"And Noah ordained them for himself as feasts for the generations forever, so that they have become thereby a memorial unto him. And on the new moon of the first month [Nisan 1, the first day of spring] he was bidden to make for himself an ark, and on that day the earth became dry and he opened the ark and saw the earth." *Ancient Book of Jubilees 6:24-25*

# Passover

The Festival of Passover occurs on Tuesday, Nisan 14, each year. The Passover lamb depicts the death of the Messiah for our sins. John the Baptist points this out in John 1:29.

> "The next day John seeth Jesus coming unto him, and saith, Behold the Lamb of God, which taketh away the sin of the world." *John 1:29*

The apostle Paul taught that we should remember the Messiah's sacrifice and focus on righteousness and repentance. The leaven represented sin and we should purge ourselves of sin.

> "Purge out therefore the old leaven, that ye may be a new lump, as ye are unleavened. For even Christ our passover is sacrificed for us: Therefore let us keep the feast, not with old leaven, neither with the leaven of malice and wickedness; but with the unleavened bread of sincerity and truth." *1 Corinthians 5:7-8*

### The Temple Ritual

In the time of Jesus, the high priest, on the 10th of Nisan, would go to Bethany to choose an unblemished lamb and bring it into the temple to be inspected for four days. As the lamb was brought to the Eastern Gate, pilgrims would line the sides of the road leading to the gate and wave the palm branches and say "Baruch Ha Shem Adonai," which means "blessed is he who comes in the name of the Lord," quoted from Psalm 118:26-27. At 9 AM on the fourteenth of Nisan, the lamb was tied to one of the horns of the altar. At 3 PM, the high priest would slay the lamb while saying the words, "it is finished."

### How Jesus Fulfilled the Passover

The temple ritual teaches us about the Messiah's death. Jesus left the house of Lazarus in Bethany on Nissan 10 to teach in the temple. There the scribes asked their hardest questions of Jesus and walked away saying "never a man spoke as this man." So, Jesus was without blemish. Jesus was hung on the cross at 9 AM and died at 3:00 PM, or "between the evenings" on Nissan 14. He acted as both priest and sacrifice when He said, "It is finished," and then died.

# Unleavened Bread

Unleavened Bread is a seven-day festival that occurs from Wednesday, Nisan 15 through Tuesday, Nisan 21. During this festival Jesus was buried and resurrected three days later.

Passover occurs on Tuesday, Nisan 14, every year. Jesus predicted that He would be in the grave for three days and three nights. On the Essene calendar Jesus would have celebrated the Last Supper with His disciples on Passover, Tuesday evening, Nisan 14. Later that night He would have been arrested, tried, and convicted of blasphemy. He would have been crucified the next day, which would have been Wednesday. Jesus would have been in the grave the three days and three nights; lasting from Wednesday night to Saturday night.

> "For as Jonas was three days and three nights in the whale's belly; so shall the Son of man be three days and three nights in the heart of the earth."
> *Matthew 12:40*

When the women went to the tomb on Sunday morning, Nisan 19, He was already risen.

So, the Festival of Unleavened Bread teaches us to put away sin. Jesus fulfilled His part of the prophecies by dying for our sins and resurrecting.

# First Fruits of the Barley Harvest

On the Essene calendar the First Fruits of the Barley Harvest occurs on Sunday, Nisan 26, each year. I was taught that this festival was on the Sunday following Passover. The Essenes, by connecting the Festivals of Passover and Unleavened Bread, taught it was the Sunday following the week of Unleavened Bread. If Jesus resurrected on Resurrection Sunday, Nisan 19, what does the Festival of the First Fruits of the Barley Harvest prophetically teach?

"But now is Christ risen from the dead, and become the firstfruits of them that slept." *1 Corinthians 15:20*

On Resurrection Sunday Jesus told Mary not to touch Him, probably because the offering was not completed in some way.

"Jesus said to her, Do not touch Me, for I have not yet ascended to My Father. But go to My brothers and say to them, I am ascending to My Father and your Father, and My God, and your God."
*John 20:17 LITV*

Later, He appeared to His disciples and told them to touch Him and see His flesh was real.

117

"Then He said to Thomas, Bring your finger here and see My hands, and bring your hand and thrust into My side, and be not unbelieving, but believing."
*John 20:27 LITV*

So, it is thought that Jesus died on Passover, was buried on the first day of Unleavened Bread. He resurrected the Sunday during the seven-day Festival of Unleavened Bread and presented atonement before the Father on the Festival of First Fruits. Jesus would have then appeared to the disciples and stated for them to touch Him because the atonement was complete. I believe our salvation was finished at the cross when Jesus said, "It is finished." I believe atonement here means ritually completed as it does when the grape and olive harvests are done, and the grapes and olives are said to be "atoned for." The meaning of this was that the first fruits were tithed, and everyone could now partake of the crops. We can see this kind of atonement is to set apart people or things for holy service. See Exodus 29:33. The altar (Exodus 29:37) and the tabernacle with the sanctuary (Leviticus 16:33) were atoned for in this manner.

# Pentecost

The Jews held the three pilgrimage Festivals of Passover, Pentecost, and Tabernacles to be the most important. Among these, the Essenes held Pentecost as the single most important festival. Pentecost is the fiftieth day after the First Fruits of the Barley Harvest. In Hebrew it is called Shavuot. The word "sheva" means seven, week, or an oath. When a word is feminine plural, the Hebrew language adds "ot" to the end. Shavuot is usually translated as the festival of "weeks." I always assumed that it should be thought of as the Festival of Weeks because of the fifty-day count, but according to the Essenes there were *four* first-fruit festivals each having a fifty-day count. They taught Shavuot should be thought of as the "Festival of the Oaths." This was the time when God entered into covenants with people.

Shavuot, or Pentecost, was always on Sunday, Sivan 15 each year. According to the Essene calendar God entered, or will enter, into the following covenants on Pentecost:

1. Adamic Covenant, Pentecost ~ pre-Flood
2. Noahide Covenant, Pentecost 1657 AM
3. Abrahamic Covenant, Pentecost 2018 AM
4. Mosaic Covenant, Pentecost 2448 AM
5. Covenant of Grace, Pentecost 3957 AM
6. Millennial Covenant, Pentecost 6000 AM

The *Ancient Book of Jubilees 6* gives details about the Festival of Oaths:

> "...it is ordained ...that they should celebrate the feast of weeks [oaths] in this month once a year, to renew the covenant every year. And this whole festival was celebrated in heaven from the day of creation till... the day of Noah's death his sons did away with it until the days of Abraham... But Abraham... Isaac and Jacob and his children observed it... in thy days the children of Israel forgot it until ye celebrated it anew on this mountain... For it is the feast of weeks and the feast of first-fruits: this feast is twofold..." *Ancient Book of Jubilees 6:17-21*

Jubilees teaches that there was some covenant between God and Adam that existed and was celebrated on Pentecost in the pre-flood world. God gave the Noahide Covenant as recorded in Genesis 9 and the Law of Kings 9 which included the seven Noahide laws, the 364-day solar calendar, and the four Days of Remembrance.

God entered into a covenant with Abraham as recorded in Genesis 12 and God entered into the Sinai covenant with the children of Israel through Moses, both on Pentecost Sundays. The Holy Spirit was given for those in the New Covenant of Grace. If the Essenes are right, the new Millennial Covenant will be given on the first Pentecost after the Second Coming and the establishment of the Millennial Kingdom.

## Daniel's Pentecost Comment

In Daniel 12, the prophet mentions two mysterious numbers, 1290 days and 1335 days. He states they are "moedim" calculations, which means that they represent the number of days between festivals, like the First Fruits of the Barley Harvest to Pentecost is fifty days.

> "And I heard the man clothed in linen, which was upon the waters of the river, when he held up his right hand and his left hand unto heaven, and sware by Him that liveth for ever that it shall be for a time, times, and an half; and when he shall have accomplished to scatter the power of the holy people, all these things shall be finished." *Daniel 12:7*

The word in this verse for time and times is "moed" and "moedim," respectively. The normal word for year is "shannah." So, Daniel is telling us the following numbers of days are between festivals. They are still three- and one-half years long but they should start and end on festivals. Many people have tried to make these two numbers fit and they just do not fit between any two festivals! That is, *if* you use the modern Jewish calendar. Notice how Daniel gives the reference. He makes it into an idiom.

> "Blessed is he who waits and comes to the thousand, three hundred and thirty-five days."
> *Daniel 12:12 LITV*

"The 1335" has a specific meaning we have never been taught. On the Dead Sea Scroll calendar there is only one place where one 1,335 days fit between two festivals. That works out only if you start on a Tabernacles and end on a Pentecost.

So, Pentecost is when we rededicate ourselves to God for the covenant of our age and "the 1335" is an idiom Daniel uses to refer to entering into a covenant at a Pentecost. In saying you are blessed if you make it to a "1335," Daniel means that those who miss the Rapture and make it through the tribulation period will be blessed if they make it to the Pentecost following Christ's Second Coming. They will enter into the kingdom covenant.

**Yearly Re-Dedication**

What I find most fascinating is that the Essenes held a very solemn ritual every year to rededicate themselves to God and the coming New Covenant of the Age of Grace. I wish every Christian would take this to heart and consider repenting of sins committed during the year and rededicating their lives and family to God and His Word every Pentecost!

# Summer Day of Remembrance

The summer Day of Remembrance always fell on Wednesday, Tammuz 1. Noah ordained this festival for the same purpose of gathering with family for feasting, repentance, and the study of prophecy. The summer Day of Remembrance specifically recalled the time when the waters of Noah's Flood were stopped.

"And on the new moon of the fourth month the mouths of the depths of the abysses beneath were closed." *Ancient book of Jubilees 6:24a*

All Days of Remembrance are for family gatherings, repentance, and studying prophecy.

123

# New Wine

The Festival of the First Fruits of New Wine occurs on Sunday, Av 3, each year. Wine symbolizes the Holy Spirit.

The only Scripture that refers to this festival is in Judges 21. After the war between Benjamin and the other tribes, the tribes swore an oath to never give their daughters in marriage to anyone from the tribe of Benjamin. The tribe of Benjamin had to get wives from somewhere or they would cease to exist. The other tribes of Israel realized their rash oath and came up with a solution to correct their mistake. The Feast of New Wine was not only a celebration for the grape harvest, but also a time for weddings. On that day a couple could get married without parental consent.

> "Then they said, Behold, there is a feast of the LORD in Shiloh yearly... Therefore they commanded the children of Benjamin, saying, Go and lie in wait in the vineyards; And see, and, behold, if the daughters of Shiloh come out to dance in dances, then come ye out of the vineyards, and catch you every man his wife of the daughters of Shiloh, and go to the land of Benjamin." *Judges 21:19-21*

This avoided the oath and allowed the Benjamites to marry. This is also a picture of the Messiah snatching away His bride at the Rapture of the church.

I think the First Fruits of New Wine uses the images of wine and marriage to teach the Holy Spirit indwelt believer needs to come to a realization that he or she needs to be completely dedicated to God. Paul says we have the first fruits of the Spirit now, but we are still waiting for the Resurrection / Rapture.

"And not only they, but ourselves also, which have the firstfruits of the Spirit, even we ourselves groan within ourselves, waiting for the adoption, to wit, the redemption of our body." *Romans 8:23*

The Jewish wedding ceremony symbolizes a total dedication, or entire sanctification, to only one spouse. Jesus is wholly sanctified to His bride, the church. We, His church, should be wholly sanctified to Christ.

"And the very God of peace sanctify you wholly; and I pray God your whole spirit and soul and body be preserved blameless unto the coming of our Lord Jesus Christ." *1 Thessalonians 5:23*

"And He said, 'For this reason a man shall leave father and mother, and shall be joined to his wife, and the two shall become one flesh.' So that they are no longer two, but one flesh. Therefore, what God has joined together, let not man separate." *Matthew 19:5-6 LITV*

New Wine is on Sunday, Av 3. Jesus went to a wedding in Cana and turned the water into wine on the Festival of New Wine. This cannot be a coincidence.

> "And the <u>third day</u> there was a marriage in Cana of Galilee; and the mother of Jesus was there:" *John 2:1*

The washing of water by the Word, mentioned in Ephesians 5:26, and the marriage supper of the Lamb both show the concept of dedication.

The 144,000 are wholly dedicated to the Messiah and have no relationship with the daughters of the Babylonian harlot. They are a first fruits, not of the barley harvest but of the New Wine grape harvest.

> "These are they which were not defiled with women; for they are virgins. These are they which follow the Lamb whithersoever He goeth. These were redeemed from among men, being the firstfruits unto God and to the Lamb." *Revelation 14:4*

The Babylonian mystery religion drinks of the wine of God's wrath. This may seem like the opposite of dedication, but look at it this way. The nations are not wholly dedicated to the Messiah as His bride. They are wholly dedicated to Mystery Babylon or one of her daughters. This is why it is called spiritual fornication.

> "For all nations have drunk of the wine of the wrath of her fornication, and the kings of the earth have

126

committed fornication with her, and the merchants of the earth are waxed rich through the abundance of her delicacies." *Revelation 18:3*

This dedication may also reflect on both Jews and Gentiles (Hebrew Roots and Noahides) becoming one new man in Christ.

"For He is our peace, who hath made both one, and hath broken down the middle wall of partition between us; Having abolished in His flesh the enmity, even the law of commandments contained in ordinances; for to make in Himself of twain one new man, so making peace; And that He might reconcile both unto God in one body by the cross, having slain the enmity thereby:" *Ephesians 2:14-16*

**Conclusion**

The Festival of New Wine teaches about our dedication to God, the marriage supper of the Lamb, the Jewish wedding ceremony, the Rapture of the church, and the new body of Christ being made of what were Jews and Gentiles.

# New Oil

The Festival of the First Fruits of New Oil occurs on Sunday, Elul 22, every year. Oil is used in lamps to create light. Oil was also used to anoint kings, priests and temple utensils to make them holy. James 5:14 says the elders of the church are to anoint the sick with oil. James also refers to God as the "Father of lights" in connection to a First Fruits Festival.

> "Every good gift and every perfect gift is from above and comes down from the Father of lights, with whom is no variableness nor shadow of turning. Of His own will He brought us forth with the Word of truth, for us to be a certain first fruit of His creatures."
> *James 1:17-18 MKJV*

**Parables of Jesus**
In Matthew 25 Jesus gives three parables, the ten virgins, the talents, and the judgment of the sheep and goats.

In the parable of the ten virgins, all ten virgins were expecting the bridegroom to come. The five wise had vessels of extra oil as well as in their lamps symbolizing that they were mature. The five foolish virgins never got around to buying any extra oil for their lamps, showing that they were not truly prepared for the Lord's coming. The oil in the lamps symbolizes letting our light shine with the

Gospel and being prepared for His coming which requires we study prophecy.

In the parable of the talents, two are faithful servants who expanded the kingdom of God, and one did nothing to expand the kingdom. The two were rewarded but the one was punished.

In the parable of the sheep and the goats, the sheep were those who dedicated themselves to Messiah and followed His teachings, while the goats were those who were Christians in name only and refused to follow Christ's teachings.

## Light of the Gospel

Compare how Second Peter and the Testament of Levi describe light. The light of the Gospel comes from the sun of righteousness and it shines to all the Gentile nations.

"His star will arise in heaven, as a king shedding forth the light of knowledge in the sunshine of day, and He will be magnified in the world until His ascension. He will shine forth as the sun in the earth, and will drive away all darkness from the world under heaven... In His priesthood the Gentiles will be multiplied in knowledge on the earth and enlightened through the grace of the Lord."
*Testament of Levi 18*

I believe Peter connects this priesthood of Gentiles, which is the Christian church, to the Festival of New Oil when he says:

> "We have also a more sure word of prophecy; whereunto ye do well that ye take heed, as unto a light that shineth in a dark place, until the day dawn, and the day star arise in your hearts:" *2 Peter 1:19*

The patriarchs teach that this synagogue of the Gentiles (the church) will have its own set of holy books (the New Testament). It will contain a series of epistles written from a Benjamite (the apostle Paul) and his history (the book of Acts). These will give us the answers we need for the Age of Grace. The New Testament will continue to exist and be used throughout all the other ages.

> "One will rise up from my seed in the latter times, beloved of the Lord, hearing His voice on the earth, enlightening with new knowledge all the Gentiles, bursting in on Israel for salvation with the light of knowledge, and tearing it away from them like a wolf, and giving it to the synagogue of the Gentiles. Until the consummation of the ages he will be in the synagogues of the Gentiles, and among their rulers, as a strain of music in the mouth of all; and he will be inscribed in the holy books, both his work and his word, and he will be a chosen one of God forever;" *Testament of Benjamin 11*

Jesus said,

"Ye are the light of the world. A city that is set on an hill cannot be hid. Neither do men light a candle, and put it under a bushel, but on a candlestick; and it giveth light unto all that are in the house. Let your light so shine before men, that they may see your good works, and glorify your Father which is in heaven." *Matthew 5:14-16*

The apostle John said,

"But if we walk in the light, as he is in the light, we have fellowship one with another, and the blood of Jesus Christ His Son cleanseth us from all sin."
*1 John 1:7*

The process from the new birth to spiritual maturity is:

1. Born of the Spirit (First Fruits of Barley Harvest)
2. New nature given by the Holy Spirit (Pentecost, First Fruits of Wheat)
3. After maturing, totally commit your walk to Christ, and become one new body, neither Jew nor Greek but Christian (New Wine, First Fruits of Grapes)
4. Letting your light shine, witnessing (New Oil, First Fruits of Olives) God is now working through the Gentile Synagogue (Church) with the New Covenant and the New Testament holy books. We focus on prophecy.

131

**Conclusion**

The main idea of this festival of light is that we need the Word of God to grow to maturity. We specifically need to study prophecy focusing on the Rapture and the Millennial kingdom. The Festival of New Oil teaches us about the new Gentile church, the New Testament, spreading the Gospel, and later our physical glorification in the Rapture.

# Wood Offering

The Festival of New Oil is Sunday Elul 22. The day after begins the weeklong wood offering. Each day two tribes were to bring a tithe of wood for the next years sacrifices. This lasts from Monday, Elul 23 to Saturday, Elul 28.

- Levi and Judah were to bring their offering on Monday Elul 23,
- Benjamin and Joseph, on Tuesday,
- Reuben and Simeon, on Wednesday,
- Issachar and Zebulun, on Thursday,
- Gad and Asher, on Friday,
- Dan and Naphtali, on Saturday, the Sabbath.

Little is known about the wood offering. There might have been rituals that accompany the offerings of wood, but none are known. This holy day may or may not be prophetic.

# Fall Day of Remembrance

The fall Day of Remembrance always fell on Wednesday, Tishrei 1. This is the same day as the Feast of Trumpets. Noah ordained this feast for family gatherings including studies in prophecy and personal repentance before God. This Day of Remembrance commemorates when the waters of the Flood began to recede.

> "And on the new moon of the seventh month all the mouths of the abysses of the earth were opened, and the waters began to descend into them."
> *Ancient Book of Jubilees 6:24b*

# Feast of Trumpets

The Feast of Trumpets occurs on Wednesday, Tishrei 1, each year. One name for this festival is "Yom Teruah" which means "the day of the awakening blast." It is taken from Numbers 29:1.

> "And in the seventh month, on the first day of the month, ye shall have an holy convocation; ye shall do no servile work: it is a <u>day of blowing the trumpets</u> [Yom Teruah] unto you." *Numbers 29:1*

The Hebrew for the words "day of blowing of trumpets" is literally Yom Teruah, the day of the awakening blast. Teruah is an awakening blast from the shofar that would be the signal for an army to wake up and prepare for the day's battle. Teruah is also translated "shout." The rabbis took this to mean this is the day of the resurrection of the dead.

### The Last Trump
Another name for this festival is the festival of "the last trump." The rabbis taught this was to be the day of the Resurrection. The apostle Paul said the Resurrection and Rapture happen at the same time.

> "In a moment, in the twinkling of an eye, at the last trump: for the trumpet shall sound, and the dead shall be raised incorruptible, and we shall be changed."
> *1 Corinthians 15:52*

135

This festival may picture the Rapture / Resurrection of believers prior to the seven-year tribulation period.

### Day of Concealment ~ Yom HaKeseh

Another name for the Feast of Trumpets is "the Day of Concealment." In Hebrew it is "Yom HaKeseh." The term was taken from Psalm 81:3 by the ancient rabbis.

> "Blow up the trumpet in the new moon, in the time appointed, on our solemn feast day." *Psalm 81:3*

The Hebrew word "Keseh" is translated "time appointed" in this passage, but actually means to conceal. This is yet another picture of the concealment of the church by the Rapture.

### Day of the King ~ HaMelek

Rosh Hashanah is also called Yom HaMelek, or the Day of the King. It is the time of Messiah's coronation and the beginning of His kingdom. Compare this to passages like Daniel 7:13-14 and Revelation 5:1-14.

If a new king was to be crowned that year, the coronation would occur on the festival of Rosh Hashanah. When this happened, Psalm 45 was read. A King always has his bride with him at his coronation.

### Day of Remembrance ~ Yom HaZikkaron

Another title for this day is Yom HaZikkaron, which means "Day of Remembrance." The rabbis took this name from

Leviticus 23:24. It is a memorial day. The word for memorial in this passage is "zikkaron" or remembrance.

> "Speak unto the children of Israel, saying, In the seventh month, in the first day of the month, shall ye have a sabbath, a memorial of blowing of trumpets, an holy convocation." *Leviticus 23:24*

This is an ancient memory of the four "Days of Remembrance" commanded by Noah to his children. The Feast of Trumpets falls on the fall Day of Remembrance.

**Days of Awe ~ Yamin Noraim**
One interesting fact is that this festival is a two day festival, which means the days between Trumpet and Yom Kippur (the third through the ninth) are called the Yamin Noraim, which means "the days of awe." This name is taken from the prophet Joel.

> "...for the day of the LORD is great and very terrible; and who can abide it?" *Joel 2:11b*

The rabbis said that these terrible days were the same as the time of Jacob's trouble.

If the Rapture were to occur on this festival, since it is a two day festival, no one could possibly know the exact day or hour it would occur!

# Day of Atonement

The Day of Atonement occurs on Friday, Tishrei 10, each year. If we see Yom Teruah as the Rapture / Resurrection and the Yamin Noraim as the seven-year tribulation period, then Yom Kippur should teach on the Second Coming.

## Ritual of the Two Goats

During the Festival of Yom Kippur there is a prophetic ceremony that involves two goats. Two nearly identical goats are selected and brought before the high priest. The high priest places his hands on one of the goats. Another priest brings out the Qalephi, a box containing two lots. One of the lots is randomly withdrawn by the high priest and placed with the first goat. The other is then withdrawn for the second goat. On one lot is engraved "for the Lord." The goat that randomly acquired the lot "for the Lord" is sacrificed for the sins of the people. This animal is a perfect representation of the Messiah dying for the sins of the world. The other lot is engraved with "for Azazel." This has commonly been translated "scapegoat," but Azazel actually is a proper name. Moses wrote about this ceremony in Leviticus 16 saying:

> "And Aaron shall cast lots upon the two goats; one lot for the LORD, and the other lot for the scapegoat. And Aaron shall bring the goat upon which the LORD'S lot fell, and offer him for a sin offering. But the goat, on which the lot fell to be the scapegoat,

shall be presented alive before the LORD, to make an atonement with him, and to let him go for a scapegoat [to Azazel] into the wilderness."
*Leviticus 16:8-10*

The Mishnah is a book written about AD 200. It contains the Oral Torah, or the exact details explaining how to perform the rituals described in the Old Testament. In Yoma 4.2 of the Mishnah, details are given concerning the ceremony of the two goats.

A scarlet-colored wool cord was specially created for this ceremony. One piece of this cord was tied to one of the horns of the Azazel goat. One piece of the cord was tied around the neck of the Lord's goat.

Leviticus describes the Azazel goat being sent into the "wilderness." But the Mishnah gives greater detail about that part of the ritual in Yoma 6. The two goats must be alike in appearance, size, and weight. The "wilderness" that the Azazel goat was taken to was actually a ravine twelve miles east of Jerusalem. Between Jerusalem and this ravine were ten stations or booths. Since it was a High Holy Day, one could not travel very far. One priest took the Azazel goat from Jerusalem to the first booth. Then another priest took it from the second to the third booth. This continued until a priest took it from the tenth booth to the ravine. Anciently this ravine was called Beit HaDudo. It still exists in the Judean desert and is presently called Jabel Muntar. The Mishnah then says the priest took the crimson cord off of the goat and tied one piece to the large rock on the cliff of the ravine, and he tied the other piece back on to the horns of the goat. He then pushed the goat off the cliff. Before it would be halfway down the cliff, it was already torn into pieces.

If the ritual was properly done, the crimson cord would turn snow white. At that point the priest would signal the tenth booth, which would in turn signal the ninth, all the way back to the first booth, which would signal the high priest standing at the door of the sanctuary. When the high priest learned the crimson thread had turned white, he finished the ritual by quoting the prophet Isaiah.

> "'Come now, and let us reason together,' saith the LORD: 'though your sins be as scarlet, they shall be as white as snow; though they be red like crimson, they shall be as wool.'" *Isaiah 1:18*

After this a massive celebration began.

### The Meaning of the Ritual

It has been speculated that the scapegoat represents Jesus taking away our sin. That is one possible interpretation. If the information given in the Mishnah is correct, another picture emerges. Two identical goats, one dedicated to God, the other dedicated to Satan. One goat represents the Messiah and the other represents the Antichrist. The only way to tell the difference between the Messiah and the Antichrist is to know the Lord's will by carefully studying the Word of God. At the Second Coming, the Antichrist

140

will be destroyed in Megiddo, in a battle called Armageddon.

## The Rest of the Ritual

Now with the rejoicing in Azazel's death, the High Priest moved forward with the rest of the ceremony. The High Priest removed the innards of the bull and the goat whose blood had been sprinkled in the Holy of Holies and placed them in a receptacle. He twisted the bodies of the two animals and four priests carried the bodies out of Jerusalem on two poles to a place called "the place of the ashes... where the bull and goat were burned only after the Azazel goat had reached the wilderness. The High Priest went into the Court of the Women and recited the eight benedictions: for the Torah, for the (sacrificial) service, for the thanksgiving, for the forgiving of sins, for the temple, for Israel, for Jerusalem, for the Kohanim (priests), and for other matters of prayer.

The High Priest then returned to the roof of the Beit HaParvah (a chamber in the temple) to remove his linen garments. He then immersed himself in the bath and put on the golden garments. He washed his hands and feet before removing one set of garments and after putting on the other. Immediately, he went to the north side of the altar, where he offered up his ram and a ram for the people as burnt offerings.

The Day of Atonement is a perfect picture of the Second Coming and the destruction of the Antichrist!

# Tabernacles

The Festival of Tabernacles occurs for seven days, between Wednesday, Tishrei 15, and Tuesday, Tishrei 21. Tabernacles is called the "Festival of Ingathering," because it begins with a great supper. The Israelites would take the second tithe and prepare a great feast. This happened every three years on the Festival of Tabernacles. See Deuteronomy 14 for details.

In the temple, seventy burnt offerings were given for the cleansing of all the Gentile nations (Numbers 29). Based on this passage the rabbis called this festival "The Festival of Nations."

**Four Species**
On the first day of Tabernacles, each man was to bring what is called the four species.

> "And ye shall take you on the first day the boughs [fruit] of goodly trees, branches of palm trees, and the boughs of thick [myrtle] trees, and willows of the brook; and ye shall rejoice before the LORD your God seven days." *Leviticus 23:40*

The Lulov is made with a tall palm branch in the center, a myrtle branch on one side, and a willow branch on the other side. These are bound together and held in the right hand. The fruit spoken of here is an etrog or yellow citron. It grows on a tree that produces fruit all year long. The fruit juice is often mixed with wine as an antidote for consuming poison.

The ritual consisted of holding the four species, the Lulov, in the right hand representing the Messiah, and the etrog upside down in the left hand, representing the Israelite and the world, backwards in sin. By the end of the ritual the etrog is right side up and joined in marriage to the Lulovim, creating the four species.

**The Sukkah**
Each Israelite family builds a tabernacle or tent, called a sukkah, out of the branches of palm, willow, myrtle, and other trees. They live in it for seven days.

"And ye shall take you on the first day the boughs of goodly trees, branches of palm trees, and the boughs of thick trees, and willows of the brook; and ye shall rejoice before the LORD your God seven days. And ye shall keep it a feast unto the LORD seven days in the year. It shall be a statute forever in your generations: ye shall celebrate it in the seventh month. Ye shall dwell in booths seven days; all that are Israelites born shall dwell in booths: that your generations may know that I made the children of Israel to dwell in booths, when I brought them out of the land of Egypt: I am the LORD your God."
*Leviticus 23:40-43*

143

**Three Stars**

One rabbinical requirement was that there be an opening in the roof of the sukkah large enough for the family members to see three stars. Genesis states we are to pay attention to the sun, moon, and stars for signs, seasons [moedim], and for days and years. If we use the proper calendar, we can accurately calculate the festivals and their future events. The star of Bethlehem is one example of a sign in the heavens.

Each day you are to have a meal with your family in the sukkah. An extra place is set for a guest. One night it is for Abraham, the next night for Isaac, then Jacob and so on. This rehearsal teaches us that in the millennium, mortals and immortals will dwell together.

"Let us be glad and rejoice, and give honour to Him: for the marriage of the Lamb is come, and His wife hath made herself ready. And to her was granted that she should be arrayed in fine linen, clean and white: for the fine linen is the righteousness of saints. And he saith unto me, write, blessed are they which are called unto the marriage supper of the Lamb. And he saith unto me, These are the true sayings of God." *Revelation 19:7-9*

This great supper is the marriage supper of the Lamb and is in contrast to the feast of Leviathan.

144

## The Feast of Leviathan

According to the Encyclopedia Judaica, Leviathan was anciently thought to be a seven-headed sea beast. It represents the Antichrist and his end time kingdom. The Feast of Leviathan is taken from Job 41.

> "Canst thou draw out leviathan with an hook?
> ...Shall the companions make a banquet of him?"
> *Job 41:1,6*

Those who follow Leviathan will be slaughtered in the Battle of Armageddon. Their flesh will be for the birds to feast on. This has also been applied to the Sheep and Goat Judgment of Matthew 25.

> "And I saw an angel standing in the sun; and he cried with a loud voice, saying to all the fowls that fly in the midst of heaven, Come and gather yourselves together unto the supper of the great God; that ye may eat the flesh of kings, and the flesh of captains, and the flesh of mighty men, and the flesh of horses, and of them that sit on them, and the flesh of all men, both free and bond, both small and great."
> *Revelation 19:17-18*

When the Egyptians were drowned in the sea, their bodies were left for the birds; likewise, the bodies of those destroyed in the battle of Armageddon will be left as food for the birds. While the church has the Marriage Supper of the Lamb, the unbelievers will take part in the Banquet of Leviathan.

Jesus says at the great trump the angels will gather the people, taking the sheep back to Jerusalem and the goats to where the eagles gather, or the Feast of Leviathan. See Matthew 24:28 and Luke 17:37.

> "Two men shall be in the field; the one shall be taken, and the other left. And they answered and said unto him, Where, Lord? And he said unto them, Wheresoever the body is, thither will the eagles be gathered together." *Luke 17:36-37*

### House of the Water Pouring - Beit HaShoevah

Beit HaShoevah is a ritual that was performed every day during Sukkot. A group of priests would gather together and go out the Eastern Gate to the Mount of Olives and from there to a valley called Motzah. They would cut willow branches, each about twenty-five feet long. The priests would then make a procession back to the temple waving the willow branches. This would create the sound of a mighty rushing wind.

While this was going on, the high priest and an assistant would leave the temple, going out through the Water Gate down to the pool of Siloam also called Siloah. The high priest would fill a golden vessel with living water from the pool and take it back to the temple. The high priest timed his reentering through the Water Gate with the procession of priests carrying the willow branches returning through the Eastern Gate. This is a prophecy that when the Messiah returns, He will come through the Eastern Gate. At that time the shofar was blown and a single flute began to play.

The man playing the flute is called "the pierced one." This was to signal both groups had returned and were about to enter the temple. At that moment another group of priests ascended the altar and began the additional animal sacrifices for that day of Sukkot.

Then the procession of priests would march around the altar seven times and lay the willow branches against the altar to form what looks like a sukkah over it. This canopy is called a "chuppah," or wedding canopy. Then the high priest with his golden vessel of living water, and his assistant with his silver vessel of sacred wine, would ascend the altar and pour both liquids together over the altar to cleanse it. At that moment the crowd witnessing this ritual would sing Isaiah 12:3.

"And in that day Thou shalt say, O LORD, I will praise Thee: though Thou wast angry with me, Thine anger is turned away, and Thou comfortedst me. Behold, God is my salvation [Yeshua]; I will trust, and not be afraid: for the LORD JEHOVAH is my strength and my song; He also is become my salvation. Therefore with joy shall ye draw water out of the wells of salvation [Yeshua]. And in that day shall ye say, Praise the LORD, call upon His name, declare His doings among the people, make mention that His name is exalted. Sing unto the LORD; for He hath done excellent things: this is known in all the earth. Cry out and shout, thou inhabitant of Zion: for great is the Holy One of Israel in the midst of thee."
*Isaiah 12:1-6*

Note that the word "salvation" here is "Yeshua" – the Hebrew name of Jesus.

The last day of Sukkot was called "the Great Day," Hoshana Rabbah. It was most likely at the time of the water pouring that Jesus stood up and called to the thirsty to come and drink.

> "In the last day, that great day of the feast, Jesus stood and cried, saying, If any man thirst, let him come unto Me, and drink. He that believeth on Me, as the scripture hath said, out of his belly shall flow rivers of living water. (But this spake He of the Spirit, which they that believe on Him should receive: for the Holy Ghost was not yet given; because that Jesus was not yet glorified.)" *John 7:37-39*

The ceremony of the Biet HaShoevah teaches about the Messianic Kingdom, the birth of the Messiah, the dedication of the temple, and the pouring of living water (water and wine) to cleanse the temple. Note Jesus' first miracle was to turn the water into wine; and He used the large stone pots that were designed for this ceremony to hold the sacred wine. Jesus turned normal water into sacred wine (or living water) showing that He was the fulfillment of this ceremony.

Zechariah predicted that all nations will be required to keep the Festival of Tabernacles, called the Festival of the Nations, during the Millennium.

"And it shall come to pass, that every one that is left of all the nations which came against Jerusalem shall even go up from year to year to worship the King, the LORD of hosts, and to keep the feast of tabernacles." *Zechariah 14:16*

# Winter Day of Remembrance

The winter Day of Remembrance always fell on Wednesday, Tevet 1.

> "And on the new moon of the tenth month the tops of the mountains were seen, and Noah was glad. And on this account, he ordained them for himself as feasts for a memorial forever, and thus are they ordained." *Ancient Book of Jubilees 6:27-28*

# Calendar Recreation?

Now that we have discovered how the ancient solar calendar works, we need to recreate it for daily use.

**How to Determine New Year's Day**
The first thing we need to do in any given year is determine when the spring equinox occurs. The spring equinox, Tekufah Nissan, is called the great sign of the start of a new year. Since we are used to the Gregorian calendar this is very easy to do. The spring equinox is almost always March 20. Once in a great while, towards the end or beginning of a century, it can fall on March 19. When writing a computer program, we would use the given calculations to determine exactly when the spring equinox occurs down to the hour and minute. But using the weekday and March 20 date as a rule of thumb, even that is not really necessary. Since we have determined that the seven-day week cycle is intact, we can just find New Year's the way it was originally designed.

The Wednesday closest to March 20 (the spring equinox) is New Year's Day, or Nisan 1. God's ways are so simple.

I have created the website dsscalendar.org. It is mobile friendly. When you go there on your phone, tablet, or PC, the first thing that you see is the Gregorian date, the Dead Sea Scroll date, and the modern Jewish date which we call the Pharisee date.

## How Dsscalendar.org Works

On dsscalendar.org we created a php back end for the website. The webpage calculates the date you load the page and gets the Gregorian day of the week, day, month, and year. It then calculates the spring equinox for that year and the previous year. If the date you loaded the page is not past the spring equinox for the current year, it uses the previous year's equinox. It then calculates the closest Wednesday to whichever spring equinox it is using and begins the calendar year.

It first adds a number to the current year to find the current Dead Sea Scroll year, then displays the AD year and the AM Year. For instance, "2020 AD" and then "5945 AM." It then adds all the Gregorian and DSS dates and the Holy Days.

The whole php program is about two and a half pages of code. If we decide that the New Year should not be calculated as the closest Wednesday to the spring equinox, but instead, on one of the other two ways discussed in the chapter on leap years, we can easily change it. The part of the code to change the start of the New year is just *five* lines of code. Enjoy.

# Appendix A
# Ancient Chronology

The year count is taken from the Bible, Jasher, Seder Olam, Enoch, and other Dead Sea Scrolls.

| | |
|---|---|
| 1 | Adam created (1-930) |
| 130 | Seth born (130-1042) |
| 235 | Enos born (235-1140) |
| 325 | Cainan born (325-1235) |
| 395 | Mahalaleel born (395-1290) |
| 460 | Jared born (460-1422) |
| 622 | Enoch born (Raptured in 987) |
| 687 | Methuselah born (687-1656) |
| 874 | Lamech born (874-1651) |
| 1056 | Noah born (1056-2006) |
| 1558 | Shem born (1558-2158) |
| 1656 | Flood occurred (Nisan 17) |
| 1658 | Arphaxad born (1658-2096) |
| 1693 | Selah born (1693-2126) |
| 1723 | Eber born (1723-2187) |
| 1757 | Peleg born (1757-1996) |
| 1787 | Reu born (1787-2026) |
| 1819 | Serug born (1819-2048) |
| 1849 | Nahor born (1849-1997) |
| 1878 | Terah born (1878-2083) |
| 1948 | Abraham born (1948-2123) |
| 2018 | Abraham's covenant |
| 2048 | Isaac born (2048-2228) |

2108  Jacob born (2108-2255)
2194  Levi born (2194-2331)
2199  Joseph born (2199-2309)
2216  Kohath born (2216-2349)
2216  Joseph enslaved
2228  Joseph becomes vice-pharaoh
2237  7-yr Famine began
2238  Jacob migrated to Egypt
2255  Jacob died
2309  Joseph died
2368  Moses born (2368-2488)
2448  Exodus from Egypt (Nisan 15)
2516  Joshua died (2406-2516)
2935  Solomon's Temple dedicated (Cheshvan 1)
3338  Solomon's Temple destroyed
3388  Cyrus' decree
3407  Darius' decree
3408  Second Temple constructed
3481  Artaxerxes' decree
3957  Crucifixion (Nisan 15)
3995  Second temple destroyed (AD 70)
5873  Israel reborn (AD 1948)
5892  Israel takes Temple Mount (AD 1967)
5898  Yom Kippur war (AD 1973)
5907  First Lebanese war (AD 1982)
5929  Sanhedrin reestablished (AD 2004)
5931  Second Lebanese war (AD 2006)
6000  Year 6000 AM (AD 2075)

# Appendix B
# Six-Year Calendar

This section is a recreation of the priestly courses of 4Q320-321. These Dead Sea Scrolls contain the basic solar calendar with each week's priestly course and the lunar phases.

The recreation has the name of the priestly course for the week, Sunday through Saturday, then lists which week of the year and month of the year that week falls in. The symbol of the full moon on the calendar is O while the new moon symbol is ☽. Whenever a second full moon occurs in one calendar month it is called a blue moon and is symbolized with ②.

# Ancient Dead Sea Scroll Calendar

## First Year

| | Sun | Mon | Tue | Wed | Thu | Fri | Sat | W | M |
|---|---|---|---|---|---|---|---|---|---|
| 1 Gamul | | | | 1○ | 2 | 3 | 4 | 1 | 1 |
| 2 Delaiah | 5 | 6 | 7 | 8 | 9 | 10 | 11 | 2 | |
| 3 Maaziah | 12 | 13 | 14 | 15 | 16 | 17☽ | 18 | 3 | |
| 4 Jehoiarib | 19 | 20 | 21 | 22 | 23 | 24 | 25 | 4 | |
| 5 Jedaiah | 26 | 27 | 28 | 29 | 30② | 1 | 2 | 5 | 2 |
| 6 Harim | 3 | 4 | 5 | 6 | 7 | 8 | 9 | 6 | |
| 7 Seorim | 10 | 11 | 12 | 13 | 14 | 15 | 16 | 7 | |
| 8 Malchijah | 17☽ | 18 | 19 | 20 | 21 | 22 | 23 | 8 | |
| 9 Mijamin | 24 | 25 | 26 | 27 | 28 | 29 | 30○ | 9 | |
| 10 Hakkoz | 1 | 2 | 3 | 4 | 5 | 6 | 7 | 10 | 3 |
| 11 Abijah | 8 | 9 | 10 | 11 | 12 | 13 | 14 | 11 | |
| 12 Jeshua | 15 | 16☽ | 17 | 18 | 19 | 20 | 21 | 12 | |
| 13 Shecaniah | 22 | 23 | 24 | 25 | 26 | 27 | 28 | 13 | |
| 14 Elishib | 29○ | 30 | | 1 | 2 | 3 | 4 | 14 | 4 |
| 15 Jakim | 5 | 6 | 7 | 8 | 9 | 10 | 11 | 15 | |
| 16 Huppah | 12 | 13 | 14 | 15☽ | 16 | 17 | 18 | 16 | |
| 17 Jeshebeab | 19 | 20 | 21 | 22 | 23 | 24 | 25 | 17 | |
| 18 Bilgah | 26 | 27 | 28○ | 29 | 30 | 1 | 2 | 18 | 5 |
| 19 Immer | 3 | 4 | 5 | 6 | 7 | 8 | 9 | 19 | |
| 20 Hezir | 10 | 11 | 12 | 13 | 14☽ | 15 | 16 | 20 | |
| 21 Happizzez | 17 | 18 | 19 | 20 | 21 | 22 | 23 | 21 | |
| 22 Pethahiah | 24 | 25 | 26 | 27○ | 28 | 29 | 30 | 22 | |
| 23 Jehezkel | 1 | 2 | 3 | 4 | 5 | 6 | 7 | 23 | 6 |
| 24 Jachin | 8 | 9 | 10 | 11 | 12 | 13 | 14☽ | 24 | |
| 1 Gamul | 15 | 16 | 17 | 18 | 19 | 20 | 21 | 25 | |
| 2 Delaiah | 22 | 23 | 24 | 25 | 26 | 27○ | 28 | 26 | |
| 3 Maaziah | 29 | 30 | | 1 | 2 | 3 | 4 | 27 | 7 |
| 4 Jehoiarib | 5 | 6 | 7 | 8 | 9 | 10 | 11 | 28 | |
| 5 Jedaiah | 12☽ | 13 | 14 | 15 | 16 | 17 | 18 | 29 | |
| 6 Harim | 19 | 20 | 21 | 22 | 23 | 24 | 25○ | 30 | |
| 7 Seorim | 26 | 27 | 28 | 29 | 30 | 1 | 2 | 31 | 8 |
| 8 Malchijah | 3 | 4 | 5 | 6 | 7 | 8 | 9 | 32 | |
| 9 Mijamin | 10 | 11 | 12☽ | 13 | 14 | 15 | 16 | 33 | |
| 10 Hakkoz | 17 | 18 | 19 | 20 | 21 | 22 | 23 | 34 | |
| 11 Abijah | 24 | 25○ | 26 | 27 | 28 | 29 | 30 | 35 | |
| 12 Jeshua | 1 | 2 | 3 | 4 | 5 | 6 | 7 | 36 | 9 |
| 13 Shecaniah | 8 | 9 | 10 | 11☽ | 12 | 13 | 14 | 37 | |
| 14 Elishib | 15 | 16 | 17 | 18 | 19 | 20 | 21 | 38 | |
| 15 Jakim | 22 | 23 | 24○ | 25 | 26 | 27 | 28 | 39 | |

156

# Appendix B - Six-Year Calendar

| | Sun | Mon | Tue | Wed | Thu | Fri | Sat | W | M |
|---|---|---|---|---|---|---|---|---|---|
| 16 Huppah | 29 | 30 | | 1 | 2 | 3 | 4 | 40 | 10 |
| 17 Jeshebeab | 5 | 6 | 7 | 8 | 9 | 10☽ | 11 | 41 | |
| 18 Bilgah | 12 | 13 | 14 | 15 | 16 | 17 | 18 | 42 | |
| 19 Immer | 19 | 20 | 21 | 22 | 23○ | 24 | 25 | 43 | |
| 20 Hezir | 26 | 27 | 28 | 29 | 30 | 1 | 2 | 44 | 11 |
| 21 Happizzez | 3 | 4 | 5 | 6 | 7 | 8 | 9☽ | 45 | |
| 22 Pethahiah | 10 | 11 | 12 | 13 | 14 | 15 | 16 | 46 | |
| 23 Jehezkel | 17 | 18 | 19 | 20 | 21 | 22○ | 23 | 47 | |
| 24 Jachin | 24 | 25 | 26 | 27 | 28 | 29 | 30 | 48 | |
| 1 Gamul | 1 | 2 | 3 | 4 | 5 | 6 | 7 | 49 | 12 |
| 2 Delaiah | 8 | 9☽ | 10 | 11 | 12 | 13 | 14 | 50 | |
| 3 Maaziah | 15 | 16 | 17 | 18 | 19 | 20 | 21 | 51 | |
| 4 Jehoiarib | 22○ | 23 | 24 | 25 | 26 | 27 | 28 | 52 | |
| | 29 | 30 | | | | | | | |

## Second Year

| | Sun | Mon | Tue | Wed | Thu | Fri | Sat | W | M |
|---|---|---|---|---|---|---|---|---|---|
| 5 Jedaiah | | | 1 | 2 | 3 | 4 | | 1 | 1 |
| 6 Harim | 5 | 6 | 7☽ | 8 | 9 | 10 | 11 | 2 | |
| 7 Seorim | 12 | 13 | 14 | 15 | 16 | 17 | 18 | 3 | |
| 8 Malchijah | 19 | 20○ | 21 | 22 | 23 | 24 | 25 | 4 | |
| 9 Mijamin | 26 | 27 | 28 | 29 | 30 | 1 | 2 | 5 | 2 |
| 10 Hakkoz | 3 | 4 | 5 | 6 | 7☽ | 8 | 9 | 6 | |
| 11 Abijah | 10 | 11 | 12 | 13 | 14 | 15 | 16 | 7 | |
| 12 Jeshua | 17 | 18 | 19 | 20○ | 21 | 22 | 23 | 8 | |
| 13 Shecaniah | 24 | 25 | 26 | 27 | 28 | 29 | 30 | 9 | |
| 14 Elishib | 1 | 2 | 3 | 4 | 5 | 6☽ | 7 | 10 | 3 |
| 15 Jakim | 8 | 9 | 10 | 11 | 12 | 13 | 14 | 11 | |
| 16 Huppah | 15 | 16 | 17 | 18 | 19○ | 20 | 21 | 12 | |
| 17 Jeshebeab | 22 | 23 | 24 | 25 | 26 | 27 | 28 | 13 | |
| 18 Bilgah | 29 | 30 | | 1 | 2 | 3 | 4 | 14 | 4 |
| 19 Immer | 5☽ | 6 | 7 | 8 | 9 | 10 | 11 | 15 | |
| 20 Hezir | 12 | 13 | 14 | 15 | 16 | 17 | 18○ | 16 | |
| 21 Happizzez | 19 | 20 | 21 | 22 | 23 | 24 | 25 | 17 | |
| 22 Pethahiah | 26 | 27 | 28 | 29 | 30 | 1 | 2 | 18 | 5 |
| 23 Jehezkel | 3 | 4☽ | 5 | 6 | 7 | 8 | 9 | 19 | |
| 24 Jachin | 10 | 11 | 12 | 13 | 14 | 15 | 16 | 20 | |
| 1 Gamul | 17○ | 18 | 19 | 20 | 21 | 22 | 23 | 21 | |
| 2 Delaiah | 24 | 25 | 26 | 27 | 28 | 29 | 30 | 22 | |

157

# Ancient Dead Sea Scroll Calendar

| | Sun | Mon | Tue | Wed | Thu | Fri | Sat | W | M |
|---|---|---|---|---|---|---|---|---|---|
| 3 Maaziah | 1 | 2 | 3 | 4☽ | 5 | 6 | 7 | 23 | 6 |
| 4 Jehoiarib | 8 | 9 | 10 | 11 | 12 | 13 | 14 | 24 | |
| 5 Jedaiah | 15 | 16 | 17○ | 18 | 19 | 20 | 21 | 25 | |
| 6 Harim | 22 | 23 | 24 | 25 | 26 | 27 | 28 | 26 | |
| 7 Seorim | 29 | 30 | | 1 | 2☽ | 3 | 4 | 27 | 7 |
| 8 Malchijah | 5 | 6 | 7 | 8 | 9 | 10 | 11 | 28 | |
| 9 Mijamin | 12 | 13 | 14 | 15○ | 16 | 17 | 18 | 29 | |
| 10 Hakkoz | 19 | 20 | 21 | 22 | 23 | 24 | 25 | 30 | |
| 11 Abijah | 26 | 27 | 28 | 29 | 30 | 1 | 2☽ | 31 | 8 |
| 12 Jeshua | 3 | 4 | 5 | 6 | 7 | 8 | 9 | 32 | |
| 13 Shecaniah | 10 | 11 | 12 | 13 | 14 | 15○ | 16 | 33 | |
| 14 Elishib | 17 | 18 | 19 | 20 | 21 | 22 | 23 | 34 | |
| 15 Jakim | 24 | 25 | 26 | 27 | 28 | 29 | 30 | 35 | |
| 16 Huppah | 1☽ | 2 | 3 | 4 | 5 | 6 | 7 | 36 | 9 |
| 17 Jeshebeab | 8 | 9 | 10 | 11 | 12 | 13 | 14○ | 37 | |
| 18 Bilgah | 15 | 16 | 17 | 18 | 19 | 20 | 21 | 38 | |
| 19 Immer | 22 | 23 | 24 | 25 | 26 | 27 | 28 | 39 | |
| 20 Hezir | 29 | 30 | ☽ | 1 | 2 | 3 | 4 | 40 | 10 |
| 21 Happizzez | 5 | 6 | 7 | 8 | 9 | 10 | 11 | 41 | |
| 22 Pethahiah | 12 | 13○ | 14 | 15 | 16 | 17 | 18 | 42 | |
| 23 Jehezkel | 19 | 20 | 21 | 22 | 23 | 24 | 25 | 43 | |
| 24 Jachin | 26 | 27 | 28 | 29☽ | 30 | 1 | 2 | 44 | 11 |
| 1 Gamul | 3 | 4 | 5 | 6 | 7 | 8 | 9 | 45 | |
| 2 Delaiah | 10 | 11 | 12○ | 13 | 14 | 15 | 16 | 46 | |
| 3 Maaziah | 17 | 18 | 19 | 20 | 21 | 22 | 23 | 47 | |
| 4 Jehoiarib | 24 | 25 | 26 | 27 | 28 | 29☽ | 30 | 48 | |
| 5 Jedaiah | 1 | 2 | 3 | 4 | 5 | 6 | 7 | 49 | 12 |
| 6 Harim | 8 | 9 | 10 | 11 | 12○ | 13 | 14 | 50 | |
| 7 Seorim | 15 | 16 | 17 | 18 | 19 | 20 | 21 | 51 | |
| 8 Malchijah | 22 | 23 | 24 | 25 | 26 | 27 | 28☽ | 52 | |
| | 29 | 30 | | 1 | 2 | 3 | 4 | | |

## Third Year

| | Sun | Mon | Tue | Wed | Thu | Fri | Sat | | |
|---|---|---|---|---|---|---|---|---|---|
| 9 Mijamin | | | | 1 | 2 | 3 | 4 | 1 | 1 |
| 10 Hakkoz | 5 | 6 | 7 | 8 | 9 | 10○ | 11 | 2 | |
| 11 Abijah | 12 | 13 | 14 | 15 | 16 | 17 | 18 | 3 | |
| 12 Jeshua | 19 | 20 | 21 | 22 | 23 | 24 | 25 | 4 | |
| 13 Shecaniah | 26 | 27☽ | 28 | 29 | 30 | 1 | 2 | 5 | 2 |

| | Sun | Mon | Tue | Wed | Thu | Fri | Sat | | |
|---|---|---|---|---|---|---|---|---|---|
| 14 Elishib | 3 | 4 | 5 | 6 | 7 | 8 | 9 | 6 | |
| 15 Jakim | 10O | 11 | 12 | 13 | 14 | 15 | 16 | 7 | |
| 16 Huppah | 17 | 18 | 19 | 20 | 21 | 22 | 23 | 8 | |
| 17 Jeshebeab | 24 | 25 | 26D | 27 | 28 | 29 | 30 | 9 | |
| 18 Bilgah | 1 | 2 | 3 | 4 | 5 | 6 | 7 | 10 | 3 |
| 19 Immer | 8 | 9O | 10 | 11 | 12 | 13 | 14 | 11 | |
| 20 Hezir | 15 | 16 | 17 | 18 | 19 | 20 | 21 | 12 | |
| 21 Happizzez | 22 | 23 | 24 | 25 | 26D | 27 | 28 | 13 | |
| 22 Pethahiah | 29 | 30 | | 1 | 2 | 3 | 4 | 14 | 4 |
| 23 Jehezkel | 5 | 6 | 7 | 8O | 9 | 10 | 11 | 15 | |
| 24 Jachin | 12 | 13 | 14 | 15 | 16 | 17 | 18 | 16 | |
| 1 Gamul | 19 | 20 | 21 | 22 | 23 | 24D | 25 | 17 | |
| 2 Delaiah | 26 | 27 | 28 | 29 | 30 | 1 | 2 | 18 | 5 |
| 3 Maaziah | 3 | 4 | 5 | 6 | 7O | 8 | 9 | 19 | |
| 4 Jehoiarib | 10 | 11 | 12 | 13 | 14 | 15 | 16 | 20 | |
| 5 Jedaiah | 17 | 18 | 19 | 20 | 21 | 22 | 23 | 21 | |
| 6 Harim | 24D | 25 | 26 | 27 | 28 | 29 | 30 | 22 | |
| 7 Seorim | 1 | 2 | 3 | 4 | 5 | 6 | 7O | 23 | 6 |
| 8 Malchijah | 8 | 9 | 10 | 11 | 12 | 13 | 14 | 24 | |
| 9 Mijamin | 15 | 16 | 17 | 18 | 19 | 20 | 21 | 25 | |
| 10 Hakkoz | 22 | 23D | 24 | 25 | 26 | 27 | 28 | 26 | |
| 11 Abijah | 29 | 30 | | 1 | 2 | 3 | 4 | 27 | 7 |
| 12 Jeshua | 5O | 6 | 7 | 8 | 9 | 10 | 11 | 28 | |
| 13 Shecaniah | 12 | 13 | 14 | 15 | 16 | 17 | 18 | 29 | |
| 14 Elishib | 19 | 20 | 21 | 22D | 23 | 24 | 25 | 30 | |
| 15 Jakim | 26 | 27 | 28 | 29 | 30 | 1 | 2 | 31 | 8 |
| 16 Huppah | 3 | 4 | 5O | 6 | 7 | 8 | 9 | 32 | |
| 17 Jeshebeab | 10 | 11 | 12 | 13 | 14 | 15 | 16 | 33 | |
| 18 Bilgah | 17 | 18 | 19 | 20 | 21D | 22 | 23 | 34 | |
| 19 Immer | 24 | 25 | 26 | 27 | 28 | 29 | 30 | 35 | |
| 20 Hezir | 1 | 2 | 3 | 4O | 5 | 6 | 7 | 36 | 9 |
| 21 Happizzez | 8 | 9 | 10 | 11 | 12 | 13 | 14 | 37 | |
| 22 Pethahiah | 15 | 16 | 17 | 18 | 19 | 20 | 21D | 38 | |
| 23 Jehezkel | 22 | 23 | 24 | 25 | 26 | 27 | 28 | 39 | |
| 24 Jachin | 29 | 30 | | 1 | 2 | 3O | 4 | 40 | 10 |
| 1 Gamul | 5 | 6 | 7 | 8 | 9 | 10 | 11 | 41 | |
| 2 Delaiah | 12 | 13 | 14 | 15 | 16 | 17 | 18 | 42 | |
| 3 Maaziah | 19D | 20 | 21 | 22 | 23 | 24 | 25 | 43 | |
| 4 Jehoiarib | 26 | 27 | 28 | 29 | 30 | 1 | 2O | 44 | 11 |
| 5 Jedaiah | 3 | 4 | 5 | 6 | 7 | 8 | 9 | 45 | |

159

# Ancient Dead Sea Scroll Calendar

| | Sun | Mon | Tue | Wed | Thu | Fri | Sat | W | M |
|---|---|---|---|---|---|---|---|---|---|
| 6 Harim | 10 | 11 | 12 | 13 | 14 | 15 | 16 | 46 | |
| 7 Seorim | 17 | 18 | 19☽ | 20 | 21 | 22 | 23 | 47 | |
| 8 Malchijah | 24 | 25 | 26 | 27 | 28 | 29 | 30 | 48 | |
| 9 Mijamin | 1 | 2○ | 3 | 4 | 5 | 6 | 7 | 49 | 12 |
| 10 Hakkoz | 8 | 9 | 10 | 11 | 12 | 13 | 14 | 50 | |
| 11 Abijah | 15 | 16 | 17 | 18☽ | 19 | 20 | 21 | 51 | |
| 12 Jeshua | 22 | 23 | 24 | 25 | 26 | 27 | 28 | 52 | |
| | 29 | 30 | | | | | | | |

## Fourth Year

| | Sun | Mon | Tue | Wed | Thu | Fri | Sat | W | M |
|---|---|---|---|---|---|---|---|---|---|
| 13 Shecaniah | | | | 1○ | 2 | 3 | 4 | 1 | 1 |
| 14 Elishib | 5 | 6 | 7 | 8 | 9 | 10 | 11 | 2 | |
| 15 Jakim | 12 | 13 | 14 | 15 | 16 | 17☽ | 18 | 3 | |
| 16 Huppah | 19 | 20 | 21 | 22 | 23 | 24 | 25 | 4 | |
| 17 Jeshebeab | 26 | 27 | 28 | 29 | 30② | 1 | 2 | 5 | 2 |
| 18 Bilgah | 3 | 4 | 5 | 6 | 7 | 8 | 9 | 6 | |
| 19 Immer | 10 | 11 | 12 | 13 | 14 | 15 | 16 | 7 | |
| 20 Hezir | 17☽ | 18 | 19 | 20 | 21 | 22 | 23 | 8 | |
| 21 Happizzez | 24 | 25 | 26 | 27 | 28 | 29 | 30○ | 9 | |
| 22 Pethahiah | 1 | 2 | 3 | 4 | 5 | 6 | 7 | 10 | 3 |
| 23 Jehezkel | 8 | 9 | 10 | 11 | 12 | 13 | 14 | 11 | |
| 24 Jachin | 15 | 16☽ | 17 | 18 | 19 | 20 | 21 | 12 | |
| 1 Gamul | 22 | 23 | 24 | 25 | 26 | 27 | 28 | 13 | |
| 2 Delaiah | 29○ | 30 | | 1 | 2 | 3 | 4 | 14 | 4 |
| 3 Maaziah | 5 | 6 | 7 | 8 | 9 | 10 | 11 | 15 | |
| 4 Jehoiarib | 12 | 13 | 14 | 15☽ | 16 | 17 | 18 | 16 | |
| 5 Jedaiah | 19 | 20 | 21 | 22 | 23 | 24 | 25 | 17 | |
| 6 Harim | 26 | 27 | 28○ | 29 | 30 | 1 | 2 | 18 | 5 |
| 7 Seorim | 3 | 4 | 5 | 6 | 7 | 8 | 9 | 19 | |
| 8 Malchijah | 10 | 11 | 12 | 13 | 14☽ | 15 | 16 | 20 | |
| 9 Mijamin | 17 | 18 | 19 | 20 | 21 | 22 | 23 | 21 | |
| 10 Hakkoz | 24 | 25 | 26 | 27○ | 28 | 29 | 30 | 22 | |
| 11 Abijah | 1 | 2 | 3 | 4 | 5 | 6 | 7 | 23 | 6 |
| 12 Jeshua | 8 | 9 | 10 | 11 | 12 | 13 | 14☽ | 24 | |
| 13 Shecaniah | 15 | 16 | 17 | 18 | 19 | 20 | 21 | 25 | |
| 14 Elishib | 22 | 23 | 24 | 25 | 26 | 27○ | 28 | 26 | |
| 15 Jakim | 29 | 30 | | 1 | 2 | 3 | 4 | 27 | 7 |
| 16 Huppah | 5 | 6 | 7 | 8 | 9 | 10 | 11 | 28 | |
| 17 Jeshebeab | 12☽ | 13 | 14 | 15 | 16 | 17 | 18 | 29 | |

160

# Appendix B - Six-Year Calendar

| | Sun | Mon | Tue | Wed | Thu | Fri | Sat | W | M |
|---|---|---|---|---|---|---|---|---|---|
| 18 Bilgah | 19 | 20 | 21 | 22 | 23 | 24 | 25O | 30 | |
| 19 Immer | 26 | 27 | 28 | 29 | 30 | 1 | 2 | 31 | 8 |
| 20 Hezir | 3 | 4 | 5 | 6 | 7 | 8 | 9 | 32 | |
| 21 Happizzez | 10 | 11 | 12☽ | 13 | 14 | 15 | 16 | 33 | |
| 22 Pethahiah | 17 | 18 | 19 | 20 | 21 | 22 | 23 | 34 | |
| 23 Jehezkel | 24 | 25O | 26 | 27 | 28 | 29 | 30 | 35 | |
| 24 Jachin | 1 | 2 | 3 | 4 | 5 | 6 | 7 | 36 | 9 |
| 1 Gamul | 8 | 9 | 10 | 11☽ | 12 | 13 | 14 | 37 | |
| 2 Delaiah | 15 | 16 | 17 | 18 | 19 | 20 | 21 | 38 | |
| 3 Maaziah | 22 | 23 | 24O | 25 | 26 | 27 | 28 | 39 | |
| 4 Jehoiarib | 29 | 30 | | 1 | 2 | 3 | 4 | 40 | 10 |
| 5 Jedaiah | 5 | 6 | 7 | 8 | 9 | 10☽ | 11 | 41 | |
| 6 Harim | 12 | 13 | 14 | 15 | 16 | 17 | 18 | 42 | |
| 7 Seorim | 19 | 20 | 21 | 22 | 23O | 24 | 25 | 43 | |
| 8 Malchijah | 26 | 27 | 28 | 29 | 30 | 1 | 2 | 44 | 11 |
| 9 Mijamin | 3 | 4 | 5 | 6 | 7 | 8 | 9☽ | 45 | |
| 10 Hakkoz | 10 | 11 | 12 | 13 | 14 | 15 | 16 | 46 | |
| 11 Abijah | 17 | 18 | 19 | 20 | 21 | 22O | 23 | 47 | |
| 12 Jeshua | 24 | 25 | 26 | 27 | 28 | 29 | 30 | 48 | |
| 13 Shecaniah | 1 | 2 | 3 | 4 | 5 | 6 | 7 | 49 | 12 |
| 14 Elishib | 8 | 9☽ | 10 | 11 | 12 | 13 | 14 | 50 | |
| 15 Jakim | 15 | 16 | 17 | 18 | 19 | 20 | 21 | 51 | |
| 16 Huppah | 22O | 23 | 24 | 25 | 26 | 27 | 28 | 52 | |
| | 29 | 30 | | | | | | | |

## Fifth Year

| | Sun | Mon | Tue | Wed | Thu | Fri | Sat | W | M |
|---|---|---|---|---|---|---|---|---|---|
| 17 Jeshebeab | | | | 1 | 2 | 3 | 4 | 1 | 1 |
| 18 Bilgah | 5 | 6 | 7☽ | 8 | 9 | 10 | 11 | 2 | |
| 19 Immer | 12 | 13 | 14 | 15 | 16 | 17 | 18 | 3 | |
| 20 Hezir | 19 | 20O | 21 | 22 | 23 | 24 | 25 | 4 | |
| 21 Happizzez | 26 | 27 | 28 | 29 | 30 | 1 | 2 | 5 | 2 |
| 22 Pethahiah | 3 | 4 | 5 | 6 | 7☽ | 8 | 9 | 6 | |
| 23 Jehezkel | 10 | 11 | 12 | 13 | 14 | 15 | 16 | 7 | |
| 24 Jachin | 17 | 18 | 19 | 20O | 21 | 22 | 23 | 8 | |
| 1 Gamul | 24 | 25 | 26 | 27 | 28 | 29 | 30 | 9 | |
| 2 Delaiah | 1 | 2 | 3 | 4 | 5 | 6☽ | 7 | 10 | 3 |
| 3 Maaziah | 8 | 9 | 10 | 11 | 12 | 13 | 14 | 11 | |
| 4 Jehoiarib | 15 | 16 | 17 | 18 | 19O | 20 | 21 | 12 | |
| 5 Jedaiah | 22 | 23 | 24 | 25 | 26 | 27 | 28 | 13 | |
| 6 Harim | 29 | 30 | | 1 | 2 | 3 | 4 | 14 | 4 |

161

# Ancient Dead Sea Scroll Calendar

| | Sun | Mon | Tue | Wed | Thu | Fri | Sat | W | M |
|---|---|---|---|---|---|---|---|---|---|
| 7 Seorim | 5☽ | 6 | 7 | 8 | 9 | 10 | 11 | 15 | |
| 8 Malchijah | 12 | 13 | 14 | 15 | 16 | 17 | 18○ | 16 | |
| 9 Mijamin | 19 | 20 | 21 | 22 | 23 | 24 | 25 | 17 | |
| 10 Hakkoz | 26 | 27 | 28 | 29 | 30 | 1 | 2 | 18 | 5 |
| 11 Abijah | 3 | 4☽ | 5 | 6 | 7 | 8 | 9 | 19 | |
| 12 Jeshua | 10 | 11 | 12 | 13 | 14 | 15 | 16 | 20 | |
| 13 Shecaniah | 17○ | 18 | 19 | 20 | 21 | 22 | 23 | 21 | |
| 14 Elishib | 24 | 25 | 26 | 27 | 28 | 29 | 30 | 22 | |
| 15 Jakim | 1 | 2 | 3 | 4☽ | 5 | 6 | 7 | 23 | 6 |
| 16 Huppah | 8 | 9 | 10 | 11 | 12 | 13 | 14 | 24 | |
| 17 Jeshebeab | 15 | 16 | 17○ | 18 | 19 | 20 | 21 | 25 | |
| 18 Bilgah | 22 | 23 | 24 | 25 | 26 | 27 | 28 | 26 | |
| 19 Immer | 29 | 30 | | 1 | 2☽ | 3 | 4 | 27 | 7 |
| 20 Hezir | 5 | 6 | 7 | 8 | 9 | 10 | 11 | 28 | |
| 21 Happizzez | 12 | 13 | 14 | 15○ | 16 | 17 | 18 | 29 | |
| 22 Pethahiah | 19 | 20 | 21 | 22 | 23 | 24 | 25 | 30 | |
| 23 Jehezkel | 26 | 27 | 28 | 29 | 30 | 1 | 2☽ | 31 | 8 |
| 24 Jachin | 3 | 4 | 5 | 6 | 7 | 8 | 9 | 32 | |
| 1 Gamul | 10 | 11 | 12 | 13 | 14 | 15○ | 16 | 33 | |
| 2 Delaiah | 17 | 18 | 19 | 20 | 21 | 22 | 23 | 34 | |
| 3 Maaziah | 24 | 25 | 26 | 27 | 28 | 29 | 30 | 35 | |
| 4 Jehoiarib | 1☽ | 2 | 3 | 4 | 5 | 6 | 7 | 36 | 9 |
| 5 Jedaiah | 8 | 9 | 10 | 11 | 12 | 13 | 14○ | 37 | |
| 6 Harim | 15 | 16 | 17 | 18 | 19 | 20 | 21 | 38 | |
| 7 Seorim | 22 | 23 | 24 | 25 | 26 | 27 | 28 | 39 | |
| 8 Malchijah | 29 | 30 | ☽ | 1 | 2 | 3 | 4 | 40 | 10 |
| 9 Mijamin | 5 | 6 | 7 | 8 | 9 | 10 | 11 | 41 | |
| 10 Hakkoz | 12 | 13○ | 14 | 15 | 16 | 17 | 18 | 42 | |
| 11 Abijah | 19 | 20 | 21 | 22 | 23 | 24 | 25 | 43 | |
| 12 Jeshua | 26 | 27 | 28 | 29☽ | 30 | 1 | 2 | 44 | 11 |
| 13 Shecaniah | 3 | 4 | 5 | 6 | 7 | 8 | 9 | 45 | |
| 14 Elishib | 10 | 11 | 12○ | 13 | 14 | 15 | 16 | 46 | |
| 15 Jakim | 17 | 18 | 19 | 20 | 21 | 22 | 23 | 47 | |
| 16 Huppah | 24 | 25 | 26 | 27 | 28 | 29☽ | 30 | 48 | |
| 17 Jeshebeab | 1 | 2 | 3 | 4 | 5 | 6 | 7 | 49 | 12 |
| 18 Bilgah | 8 | 9 | 10 | 11 | 12○ | 13 | 14 | 50 | |
| 19 Immer | 15 | 16 | 17 | 18 | 19 | 20 | 21 | 51 | |
| 20 Hezir | 22 | 23 | 24 | 25 | 26 | 27 | 28☽ | 52 | |
| | 29 | 30 | | 1 | 2 | 3 | 4 | | |

# Appendix B - Six-Year Calendar

## Sixth Year

| | Sun | Mon | Tue | Wed | Thu | Fri | Sat | W | M |
|---|---|---|---|---|---|---|---|---|---|
| 21 Happizzez | | | 1 | 2 | 3 | 4 | | 1 | 1 |
| 22 Pethahiah | 5 | 6 | 7 | 8 | 9 | 10○ | 11 | 2 | |
| 23 Jehezkel | 12 | 13 | 14☽ | 15 | 16 | 17 | 18 | 3 | |
| 24 Jachin | 19 | 20 | 21 | 22 | 23 | 24 | 25 | 4 | |
| 1 Gamul | 26 | 27☽ | 28 | 29 | 30 | 1 | 2 | 5 | 2 |
| 2 Delaiah | 3 | 4 | 5 | 6 | 7 | 8 | 9 | 6 | |
| 3 Maaziah | 10○ | 11 | 12 | 13 | 14 | 15 | 16 | 7 | |
| 4 Jehoiarib | 17 | 18 | 19 | 20 | 21 | 22 | 23 | 8 | |
| 5 Jedaiah | 24 | 25 | 26☽ | 27 | 28 | 29 | 30 | 9 | |
| 6 Harim | 1 | 2 | 3 | 4 | 5 | 6 | 7 | 10 | 3 |
| 7 Seorim | 8 | 9○ | 10 | 11 | 12 | 13 | 14 | 11 | |
| 8 Malchijah | 15 | 16 | 17 | 18 | 19 | 20 | 21 | 12 | |
| 9 Mijamin | 22 | 23 | 24 | 25 | 26☽ | 27 | 28 | 13 | |
| 10 Hakkoz | 29 | 30 | | 1 | 2 | 3 | 4 | 14 | 4 |
| 11 Abijah | 5 | 6 | 7 | 8○ | 9 | 10 | 11 | 15 | |
| 12 Jeshua | 12 | 13 | 14 | 15 | 16 | 17 | 18 | 16 | |
| 13 Shecaniah | 19 | 20 | 21 | 22 | 23 | 24☽ | 25 | 17 | |
| 14 Elishib | 26 | 27 | 28 | 29 | 30 | 1 | 2 | 18 | 5 |
| 15 Jakim | 3 | 4 | 5 | 6 | 7○ | 8 | 9 | 19 | |
| 16 Huppah | 10 | 11 | 12 | 13 | 14 | 15 | 16 | 20 | |
| 17 Jeshebeab | 17 | 18 | 19 | 20 | 21 | 22 | 23 | 21 | |
| 18 Bilgah | 24☽ | 25 | 26 | 27 | 28 | 29 | 30 | 22 | |
| 19 Immer | 1 | 2 | 3 | 4 | 5 | 6 | 7○ | 23 | 6 |
| 20 Hezir | 8 | 9 | 10 | 11 | 12 | 13 | 14 | 24 | |
| 21 Happizzez | 15 | 16 | 17 | 18 | 19 | 20 | 21 | 25 | |
| 22 Pethahiah | 22 | 23☽ | 24 | 25 | 26 | 27 | 28 | 26 | |
| 23 Jehezkel | 29 | 30 | | 1 | 2 | 3 | 4 | 27 | 7 |
| 24 Jachin | 5○ | 6 | 7 | 8 | 9 | 10 | 11 | 28 | |
| 1 Gamul | 12 | 13 | 14 | 15 | 16 | 17 | 18 | 29 | |
| 2 Delaiah | 19 | 20 | 21 | 22☽ | 23 | 24 | 25 | 30 | |
| 3 Maaziah | 26 | 27 | 28 | 29 | 30 | 1 | 2 | 31 | 8 |
| 4 Jehoiarib | 3 | 4 | 5○ | 6 | 7 | 8 | 9 | 32 | |
| 5 Jedaiah | 10 | 11 | 12 | 13 | 14 | 15 | 16 | 33 | |
| 6 Harim | 17 | 18 | 19 | 20 | 21☽ | 22 | 23 | 34 | |
| 7 Seorim | 24 | 25 | 26 | 27 | 28 | 29 | 30 | 35 | |
| 8 Malchijah | 1 | 2 | 3 | 4○ | 5 | 6 | 7 | 36 | 9 |
| 9 Mijamin | 8 | 9 | 10 | 11 | 12 | 13 | 14 | 37 | |
| 10 Hakkoz | 15 | 16 | 17 | 18 | 19 | 20 | 21☽ | 38 | |
| 11 Abijah | 22 | 23 | 24 | 25 | 26 | 27 | 28 | 39 | |

163

# Ancient Dead Sea Scroll Calendar

| | Sun | Mon | Tue | Wed | Thu | Fri | Sat | W | M |
|---|---|---|---|---|---|---|---|---|---|
| 12 Jeshua | 29 | 30 | | 1 | 2 | 3○ | 4 | 40 | 10 |
| 13 Shecaniah | 5 | 6 | 7 | 8 | 9 | 10 | 11 | 41 | |
| 14 Elishib | 12 | 13 | 14 | 15 | 16 | 17 | 18 | 42 | |
| 15 Jakim | 19☽ | 20 | 21 | 22 | 23 | 24 | 25 | 43 | |
| 16 Huppah | 26 | 27 | 28 | 29 | 30 | 1 | 2○ | 44 | 11 |
| 17 Jeshebeab | 3 | 4 | 5 | 6 | 7 | 8 | 9 | 45 | |
| 18 Bilgah | 10 | 11 | 12 | 13 | 14 | 15 | 16 | 46 | |
| 19 Immer | 17 | 18 | 19☽ | 20 | 21 | 22 | 23 | 47 | |
| 20 Hezir | 24 | 25 | 26 | 27 | 28 | 29 | 30 | 48 | |
| 21 Happizzez | 1 | 2○ | 3 | 4 | 5 | 6 | 7 | 49 | 12 |
| 22 Pethahiah | 8 | 9 | 10 | 11 | 12 | 13 | 14 | 50 | |
| 23 Jehezkel | 15 | 16 | 17 | 18☽ | 19 | 20 | 21 | 51 | |
| 24 Jachin | 22 | 23 | 24 | 25 | 26 | 27 | 28 | 52 | |
| | 29 | 30 | | | | | | | |

This re-creation of the priestly courses shows us that the Essenes recorded the moon phases to show there is no leap day each year and to prove the moon phases are not a necessary part of the original calendar.

164

# Other Books by Ken Johnson, Th.D.

- **Ancient Post-Flood History**
  Historical documents that point to a biblical Creation.

- **Ancient Seder Olam**
  A Christian translation of the 2000-year-old scroll

- **Ancient Prophecies Revealed**
  500 Prophecies listed in order of when they were fulfilled

- **Ancient Book of Jasher**
  Referenced in Joshua 10:13; 2 Samuel 1:18; 2 Timothy 3:8

- **Third Corinthians**
  Ancient Gnostics and the end of the world

- **Ancient Paganism**
  The sorcery of the fallen angels

- **The Rapture**
  The pretribulational Rapture of the church viewed from the Bible and the ancient church

- **Ancient Epistle of Barnabas**
  His life and teaching

- **The Ancient Church Fathers**
  What the disciples of the apostles taught

- **Ancient Book of Daniel**

- **Ancient Epistles of John and Jude**

- **Ancient Messianic Festivals**
  And the prophecies they reveal

- **Ancient Word of God**

- **Cults and the Trinity**

- **Ancient Book of Enoch**

- **Ancient Epistles of Timothy and Titus**

- **Fallen Angels**

- **Ancient Book of Jubilees**

- **The Gnostic Origins of Calvinism**

- **The Gnostic Origins of Roman Catholicism**

- **Demonic Gospels**

- **The Pre-Flood Origins of Astrology**

- **The End-Times by the Church Fathers**

- **Ancient Book of Gad the Seer**

- **Ancient Apocalypse of Ezra**
  Called 2 Esdras in the KJV

- **Ancient Testaments of the Patriarchs**
  Autobiographies from the Dead Sea Scrolls

- **Ancient Law of Kings**
  Noahide law

- **Ancient Origins of the Hebrew Roots Movement**
  The Noahide and Mosaic Laws as seen in the Dead Sea Scrolls

- **Ancient Origins of Modern Holidays**

- DVD 1 – **The Prophetic Timeline**

- DVD 2 – **The Church Age**


For more information,
visit us at: Biblefacts.org

# Bibliography

Ken Johnson, *Ancient Book of Jasher*, Createspace, 2013
Ken Johnson, *Ancient Seder Olam*, Createspace, 2006
Whiston, William, *The Works of Flavius Josephus*, London, Miller & Sowerby, 1987. Includes Antiquities of the Jews.
Ken Johnson, *Ancient book of Enoch*, Createspace, 2012
Mattis Kantor, *Jewish Time Line Encyclopedia*, Jason Aronson, 1993
Ken Johnson, *Ancient Testaments of the Patriarchs*, Createspace, 2017